Leni Fiedelmeier

Dachshunds
A Complete Pet Owner's
Manual

Everything about Care, Training, and Health

With 18 Color Photographs by Outstanding Animal Photographers
and 29 Drawings by Sepp Arnemann

Translated by Rita and Robert Kimber
U.S. Consulting Editor: Dr. Matthew M. Vriends, D.Sc., Ph.D.

Barron's
New York • London • Toronto • Sydney

First English language edition published in
1985 by Barron's Educational Series, Inc.
© 1981 by Gräfe and Unzer GmbH, Munich,
   West Germany
The title of the German edition is *Dackel*.

Barron's Educational Series, Inc.
250 Wireless Boulevard
Hauppauge, New York 11788

Library of Congress Catalog Card No. 84-24458
International Standard Book No. 0-8120-2888-0

Library of Congress Cataloging in Publication Data

Fiedelmeier, Leni.
   Dachshunds: everything about care, training, and
health.

   Translation of: Dackel.

   Includes index.
   1. Dachshund.   I. Title.
SF429.D25F52713   1985   636.7′53   84-24458
ISBN 0-8120-2888-0

PRINTED IN HONG KONG

789   490   9876543

Front cover: Short-haired dachshund
Inside front cover: Wirehaired dachshund
Inside back cover: Wirehaired dachshund
Back cover: Two wirehaired dachshunds

Photo credits:

Animal/Thompson: page 45
Fiedelmeier: page 17 (below right)
Schneider-Wegler: page 17 (above left and right),
      back cover
Ullmann: front cover, inside front cover, pages 17
      (below left), 18, 28, 46, 63, 64
Vogeler: page 27, inside back cover

Contents

Contents

A Word Up Front

According to the American Kennel Club (AKC), the dachshund ranks eighth in popularity polls. This is quite amazing considering that this little dog has the reputation of being exceedingly stubborn and hard—if not impossible—to train.

It is true that dachshunds are stubborn. They have to be. Being the smallest breed used for hunting, dachshunds must be plucky and independent to do their job. This is the source of their obstinacy. Why is it, though, that so many dog lovers pick a dachshund when they are looking for a family pet? The answer is that these little rascals have an irresistible charm as they keep dreaming up new tricks. It is not at all easy to resist a dachshund's innocent gaze after it has done something naughty or to scold it rather than laugh.

However, it is crucial to train a dachshund with care and consistency. This is why I have devoted so much space to the chapter on training. I have also covered all the other topics that have to do with keeping a dachshund. What you should watch out for when buying a dachshund. How you can help it get settled in its new home. What it needs to feel comfortable. I also provide you with up-to-date information on nutrition and health care.

I have kept dachshunds for twenty-five years, and they have been a great delight to me. Obviously there have also been some trying moments. With this book as an aid, you, too, should find that the good times you have with this four-footed comedian will far outweigh the less pleasant ones.

I should like to express my special thanks to Mr. Sepp Arnemann, whose humorous drawings so aptly illustrate the varied aspects of the relations between dog and human. I am also very grateful to the publishers for the careful attention with which they have edited and designed this book.

Leni Fiedelmeier

Considerations Before You Buy

Is a Dachshund Right For You?

In listings of the most popular dogs, dachshunds always appear close to the top. They are likely to be preceded only by poodles and German shepherds. This means that a great number of dog lovers decide in favor of a dachshund. It would appear, then, that no special magic is required to care for a dachshund. Granted, there are some owners of dachshunds who are at a loss as to how to deal with their pet's apparent willfulness, but this can hardly be blamed on the dog. It is usually the master who has failed from the very beginning to convey his or her wishes with sufficient emphasis. If you want to have an obedient dog but know that you are not the assertive type and have trouble imposing your will on others, you may want to think twice before you settle on a dachshund. For a dog lover with limited energy or educational talent there are various other breeds that are by nature more docile than the dachshund. You should be aware before you purchase your dog that, small though it be, a dachshund must be properly and consistently trained. You also need a good sense of humor if you want to keep a dachshund, because these dogs—especially as puppies—seem to have a boundless capacity for getting into mischief.

Another factor you should take into consideration when you decide whether to choose a dachshund is where you live. Dachshunds, especially the miniature types, are small and can easily be kept in an apartment, but a walk-up is a problem. The higher up the apartment, the greater is the problem. Why? Dachshunds are simply not built for climbing stairs. Their extremely short legs together with their long backs make for poor "transmission." Climbing stairs puts the dachshund's spine under a great strain, which can result in slipped or ruptured disks, often accompanied by partial paralysis. This condition, which is fairly common in dachshunds, is described more fully in the chapter on diseases (page 47).

One way to deal with stairs in a building without an elevator is to carry the dog, but you should think twice before you embark on this route. A standard-sized dachshund can weigh up to 20 pounds (9 kilograms). Carrying a dog that heavy is no joy, and remember that you have to do it not just on nice days but also when your dog returns wet and dirty from a walk in the rain. Carrying a miniature dachshund (weighing less than 10 pounds [4.5 kilograms]) is easier, but hardly an enjoyable chore.

Many prospective dog owners choose a dog on the basis of how much grooming a given breed requires. With respect to this criterion, there is a dachshund for every taste. Of course, no dachshund requires trimming or clipping, and you will be saved the expense of these services.

The short-haired, or smooth, dachshund obviously requires the least grooming, and the long-haired type the most. The popular wirehaired variety is between these. Choose the dog that appeals to you the most. In my opinion, the grooming that a long-haired or a wirehaired dachshund needs is no great problem. Keeping a dachshund of whatever type clean and neat takes no more than a quarter of an hour a day, and surely no dog lover will begrudge spending that much time with his or her pet.

Seven Questions Dachshund Fanciers Should Ask Themselves

I have already suggested several areas you should give some thought to *before* buying a dachshund. The other things that you should consider before getting your first dog concern not just dachshunds but are of a fundamental nature. Please answer the following questions with complete honesty:

• Are you aware that having a dog is not all pure pleasure?

• Are you not just willing but also able to

Are you prepared to react with humor and understanding even in a situation like this?

spend a considerable amount of time with your dog?

• If you live in an apartment or rent a house, do you have your landlord's written permission to keep a dog?

• Are you prepared to take at least one longish walk a day in addition to the shorter outings necessary for the dog to relieve itself?

• Do you have enough time, patience, and affection for animals to play with your dog every day?

• Are you aware that a young dog, especially a puppy, should be supervised all the time?

• Are you in a financial position to assume the expenses of keeping a dog?

In reading this book, take plenty of time to think over carefully whether you qualify as a potentially successful dog owner and whether a dachshund is the right breed for you.

Where Should You Buy?

If it is important to you to own a pure-bred dog descended from flawless stock, you should write to the Dachshund Club of America, Inc. (DCA) and ask for the local DCA address, if any, and a list of approved breeders. A purebred dachshund comes with pedigree papers, denoting its background and identity. These papers may list the dog's ancestors several generations back. If you purchase a dachshund with papers, you can be assured that you have a purebred dog that is registered in the stud book. You should also receive the dog's American Kennel Club registration certifi-

7

cate (or an application form to fill out) and a health certificate made out by the breeder's veterinarian. The AKC registration number is often tattooed in the dog's ear; in the case of mixed-breed dogs, the owner's Social Security number is generally used.

After receiving a kennel listing, take the trouble of going to several and seeing for yourself how the dogs are kept. Kennels are not inspected weekly and even recommended ones should be inspected personally. Not all breeders of dachshunds live up to the ideal kennel owner who raises dogs purely as an avocation. For this reason, I always advise prospective dog owners to buy from a small hobby breeder rather than a large kennel where the dogs are kept in runs. If you want a dog that will become your personal friend and a true family dog, a puppy that has been brought up in a run away from frequent human contact may not work out. Puppies from large kennels have little contact with people, and this becomes more noticeable the older the animal is when you purchase it. If it has spent more than twelve weeks in a kennel, it is already past its first imprinting phase. At this age, a puppy that has been raised in a home-like environment with people is usually almost completely housebroken and used to a collar and leash. This considerably facilitates the further training of the dog. All the puppies I have raised grew up as part of our family, and the buyers were always very pleased at the friendliness of their newly purchased pets.

Some people object to the idea of a long trip just to inspect a kennel, but keep in mind that your dog may, if all goes well, share your life for twelve to fifteen years. You therefore cannot be too careful in choosing your four-footed housemate. It is neither a machine nor a household gadget that can be exchanged if you are not fully satisfied. To be sure, there are situations in which you must conclude, even after the most painstaking planning, that things are not working out and that the new member of the household you had so looked forward to, must go. Then you must show enough consideration for the animal to find another good home for it and not to simply get rid of it.

Cases of basic incompatibility should be rare exceptions, however, and to prevent your situation from becoming such an exception I want to stress once more: think first, then think again, and only then buy, weighing every factor carefully.

Beware of Buying on Impulse

No lover of animals in immune to the temptation to buy a pet on impulse. Such ill-considered, spur-of-the-moment purchases are most likely to occur when we see puppies displayed in some storefront window and, overcome with pity, want to rescue at least one of them. You should understand that such purchases involve a risk. These young dogs often come from large, commercial kennels where puppies are produced almost like merchandise. Such animals are often in poor health, so if you do buy a puppy out of pity, be sure to take it to a veterinarian first thing for a thorough check-up.

Considerations Before You Buy

The story is different if you buy your puppy from a reputable retail pet store or the pet section of a department store. The majority of these animals come from respected kennels, have the necessary immunizations and papers, and are generally under veterinary supervision.

If you are looking through newspaper advertisements to find a dachshund, disregard any notices that offer "dogs of any breed" for sale or claim even a number of breeds "from our own kennels." It is true that some serious breeders raise two, three, or, in exceptional cases, even four different breeds of dogs. In this case it is important to check whether the kennel owner belongs to the AKC-recognized dog clubs of the breeds in question. If so, you have some assurance that the puppies will be of good quality. You have only some assurance, however, not complete assurance. That is why I always urge so strongly, never have a puppy sent to you that you have not personally inspected at the kennel and whose mother you have not seen. Even if the puppy is too young at the time of your visit for you to take it with you and you want to have it shipped to you when it is old enough, this is not an ideal solution for the following reasons:

• Puppies are often traumatized by the shock of being torn from their familiar surroundings, locked in a crate all alone, and sent on a long trip.
• You can never be certain exactly how long anything will be in transit, even if it is shipped express, nor can you know where crates will be placed when they are unloaded and reloaded.
• There is no way of telling how the shock of being shipped will affect the puppy. Even a trip that goes quite smoothly often leaves a mark on the puppy's psyche that may later be reflected in the dog's personality.

These are the reasons I have always refused to ship puppies I have raised. Anyone who was unwilling to pick up in person was automatically disqualified as a buyer. Here, by the way, is a rule for you to go by: the more thoroughly a breeder quizzes you—the more he or she wants to know about where the puppies are going to live and how much you know about keeping dogs—the more confident you can be

Buying a dog is a matter of trust. Your best bet is to buy from a breeder recommended by the Dachshund Club of America.

that everything possible was done to raise the puppies well. If you run into breeders who are eager to sell their "product" for as much money as possible, be sure to inspect the general condition of the animals in the kennel and to observe the behavior of the older dogs. If they act shy and fearful and seem to have no real contact with people, this is a clear sign that you should not do business there.

Remember, do not neglect to make inquiries, get addresses of different breeders, and visit the kennels. No effort is too great if you want to "live happily ever after" with your four-legged friend.

How to Choose a Puppy

Now that you have gotten the addresses and perhaps visited several kennels, you have decided where you are going to buy. If the puppies have already been born, you may have had a chance to see the litter. This is not too likely, though, if the puppies are under three weeks old, because a visit by a stranger would upset the mother too much. Anyway, a novice dog fancier would benefit little from such an early visit because at this stage the puppies are not much more than cute little fur balls. You cannot detect any differences in behavior until they start to play. (The breeder, of course, who spends time with them every day, will recognize very early which members of the litter are the strongest and most determined from the way the little creatures approach the mother for nursing.)

Play—which is nothing less than practice for the serious business of life—reveals a great deal about the puppies and their per-

sonalities. You must watch them quietly and unobtrusively, leaving them alone and not interfering in any way. You will soon be able to tell which one is the leader and which ones hold back, play only cautiously, or refuse to join in the game altogether. The older the puppies are, the more pronounced the differences among them. The same is obviously true of physical differences, too.

Now you have to ask yourself what kind of personality you favor. Do you prefer a dog with a will of its own (which it eventually will pit against yours, needless to say) or a more docile type that will probably be easier to train? Perhaps you want a

At first glance, all dachshund puppies look alike. If you observe them for a while, however, you will be able to recognize differences even at this early age.

small, plucky dog that never passes up a fight. Such dogs exist, and they are quite easy to recognize as puppies. Then you should be prepared for dog fights, some unpleasant scenes, and, most likely, veterinarians' bills. At the opposite end of the

Considerations Before You Buy

scale is the excessively timid type, which also has its problems. Quite apart from the fact that excessively timid dogs often develop into nippers out of sheer fear, it is no fun having to worry constantly about a dog's shaky nerves.

How can you tell if a puppy is excessively fearful? A young dog that is at ease with people should come up to you without great hesitation. It should not shy back when you touch it, though you should approach slowly and calmly and not just grab it. In other words, the dog should not retreat into a corner and growl when you approach, nor should it snap at your hand. I want to stress again: these rules apply only to puppies that are used to people.

Young dogs that have had hardly any contact with humans must be judged differently. Suspicion and caution characterize their behavior. They have to familiarize themselves with people first and learn slowly to trust them. Still, you can detect basic character differences even in dogs brought up in a run if you have a chance to observe them long enough. You can spot the tough guy, the future pack leader, just as quickly as its more timid, self-effacing littermate. These observations will help you predict your dog's basic personality when it is still young.

The question remains: what is the best age at which to bring your puppy home? As a basic rule I would say, the less you know about dogs, the older the puppy should be. In no event, however, should it be less than ten weeks old. No breeder who agrees readily to hand over an eight-week-old puppy can possibly be very concerned about the well-being of his or her charges. On the other hand, a puppy should preferably not be over twelve weeks old, especially if it was raised exclusively in a run. Three months is the ideal age for it to be introduced to its family. Of course, it is trying to have such a young, inexperienced little creature that has not the faintest idea of how a family dog is supposed to behave. You will need a lot of time to devote to your new charge. If you do not have the time, you would do better to give up the idea of having a puppy, or those early weeks will be a nightmare for both you and the dog.

In the case of a wirehaired dachshund, there is one more question to be answered that is purely a matter of taste: do you want a dog that conforms to the official standard (page 21), or do you prefer one with a tousled look? You may ask, is there a difference? Indeed, there is. According to the standard, a wirehaired dachshund should look almost identical to its short-haired cousin. The only difference is that its coat should be short, tight, thick, rough, and hard, and it should have a beard and bushy eyebrows. The kind of dog over whom the layperson exclaims, "Oh, how cute!" rarely has the type of coat prescribed by the standard. I have to admit that I, too, favor the tousled look, as do most lovers of this breed, unless they happen to want a show dog. You can tell even in a puppy what its fur will be like later on: the smoother the puppy's coat, the smoother it will be in the grown dog. Puppies that will grow into shaggy dogs have a bit of a beard and longer hair than do their siblings that conform more closely to the official standard.

11

Considerations Before You Buy

Should You Get a Purebred Dachshund?

If you do not care particularly about having a purebred dog, you might want to visit an animal shelter. Perhaps you will find a dachshund there just waiting for a good home, or you may find a dog you like that is not 100 percent dachshund. If your main concern is simply to find a good dog to share your life, you should decide in its favor without hesitation. At this point you may ask yourself, and me, "Well then, why bother about a purebred dog at all?"

This is a reasonable question for anybody who wants a dog just for the sake of having a dog, but anyone who has specific ideas about what a breed should be like, whether in terms of appearance or character traits and abilities, should go to the trouble of finding a purebred. After all, the breeds we have today did not come into existence overnight. Many of them have been developed for special skills. Hunting dogs—among which class the dachshund belongs—are a good example. The same can be said of purebred dogs' appearance. If you see a German shepherd or a St. Bernard, a fox terrier or a dachshund, to mention just a few, you recognize it right away.

As a general rule, both the external appearance and the special talents of a breed are determined by ancestry, and purebred dogs should be kept in a way that conforms to their special makeup. You cannot expect to keep a hunting dog in the country on a piece of land that is not fenced in. It will almost certainly go after any animal that appears within its range of vision and scent. In such a situation a house dog would be much more appropriate, perhaps a Lhasa Apso or a toy poodle. I would also never advise people to get dachshunds unless their yards are escape-proof. Considerations of this nature are in order with a purebred dog because you can predict with a high degree of accuracy what to expect. The same is not true of a mongrel where you may be in for all sorts of surprises. This is the real difference to keep in mind when deciding whether to get a purebred dog.

The other element is, of course, physical appearance. If you want a dachshund, it should look like a dachshund.

Male or Female?

Most people initially seem to prefer a male, citing the common opinion that males are easier to keep than females. Those who favor females, on the other hand, argue that they are more loyal and affectionate than males.

What are the facts? Before you decide, I would advise you to have a good look around your neighborhood. Are there more female dogs being taken for walks or more males? If the latter is the case, you, too, should settle for a male. If there are more females, on the other hand, then you are better off with a female. Why? If you keep a male in a neighborhood that is predominantly inhabited by females you are likely to run into some unpleasantness. Not every owner of a female dog takes the trouble of supplying the dog with birth-control shots or of giving her chlorophyll tablets during the heat period to suppress the odor she spreads. A healthy, normal male dog finds this scent simply irresistible and will take advantage of any opportunity to run off in pursuit. This is probably the basis of the common assumption that females are more faithful than males. Actually, a female at the height of estrus (heat)—which, of

Lifting a leg against trees and lamp posts is part of a healthy male dachshund's natural behavior. Before you choose a male, you should take this into consideration.

course, occurs no more than twice a year—is just as unreliable and disobedient as an amorous male. Needless to say, a male surrounded by a large number of females is tempted often to follow the trail of a female in heat. He will then sit in front of her door for nights on end, give up eating,

lose weight, and—if securely locked up—drive his master to distraction with his whining and yowling.

If you do choose a female there are some alternatives open to you in handling the heat problem. If you are certain that you do not wish to breed your dog, you can have her spayed (sterilized) after her second or third heat. This solves the question of heat permanently. Another possibility is to suppress heat temporarily by giving your dog hormone shots. If you choose not to do anything, then, of course, you should be prepared for the fact that your dog will be extremely attractive to all the males around.

From my extensive experience with dogs of both sexes, I cannot confirm that females are more affectionate and gentle, let alone more docile, than males. My males have been just as cuddly as my females, among which, by the way, I have encountered more than a few obstinate individuals. In short, the choice between a male and female depends entirely on your personal preference.

The Cost of Keeping a Dachshund

The first cost of dog ownership is the initial purchase price, which, of course, is an expense that does not recur. For a purebred dachshund this should come to about $250 to $350. In addition, you will have to buy basic equipment like a leash, collar, and food and water dishes as well as a number of accessories (page 24).

The prime cost is, however, the cost of food. In the case of a small dog it will not be exorbitant, but you still have to figure on about $25 a month. Then there is a yearly license fee, which varies from locality to locality.

Vaccinations and other veterinarians bills are another category of cost. If all your dog needs are yearly booster shots, including rabies shots, the cost may be no more than about $25, but even the healthiest dog gets sick occasionally or gets bitten or may need lengthy treatment. Then the bills will be of a greater magnitude. In any case, it is realistic to anticipate spending money on your dog's health.

Breed Characteristics

Names, Coat Varieties, and Sizes

The dachshund's name is German and means "badger dog." In Germany, it is known not only by this name but also as *Teckel, Tackel, Dachsel,* and *Dackel.*

Dachshunds are bred in three different coat varieties:
- Short-haired, or smooth
- Wirehaired
- Long-haired

Originally there was only one kind of dachshund, the short-haired. The long-haired and wirehaired varieties are the result of later selective breeding.

Dachshunds also come in two different basic sizes:
- Standard
- Miniature

There are two sizes of miniature dachshunds. The adult regular miniature weighs about 10 pounds (4.5 kilograms), and in Germany there is an even smaller version, called the *Kaninchenteckel* (rabbit dachshund).

Glossary

Specialized terms that are useful to know or that may be used in the text that follows are explained here.

Bolt   To drive or "start" an animal out of its earth or burrow.

Brindle   A fine, even mixture of black hairs with hairs of a lighter color, usually tan, brown, or gray.

Brush tail   A tail characterized by hair that is considered too coarse and, thus, a fault in physical conformation.

Conformation   The form and structure, make and shape; arrangement of the parts in conformance with breed-standard demands.

Croup   The part of the body over the first four tail vertebrae and the hip joints of the pelvis.

Culotte   The longer hair on the back of the thighs.

Cynology   The study of canines.

Dappled   Mottled marking of different colors, no one predominating.

Dewclaw   An extra claw or functionless digit on the inside of the leg; a rudimentary fifth toe.

Dewlap   Loose, pendulous skin under the throat.

Drag   A trail prepared by dragging along the ground a bag impregnated with animal scent, usually.

Dry   As in "dry neck"; the skin is taut, neither loose nor wrinkled.

Flag   A long tail carried high; usually referring to one of the pointing breeds.

Kink tail   The tail sharply bent (usually from birth).

Knuckling over   Faulty structure of carpus (wrist) joint, allowing it to double forward under the weight of the standing dog.

Level or pincer bite   When the front teeth (incisors) of the upper and lower jaws meet exactly edge to edge.

Muzzle   The head in front of the eyes; that is, nasal bone, nostrils, and jaws.

Overshot   The front teeth (incisors) of the upper jaw overlap and do not touch the front teeth of the lower jaw when the mouth is closed.

Plume   A long fringe of hair hanging from the tail, as in setters.

Roach back or *carp back*   A convex cur-

vature of the back toward the loin.
Rudder The tail.
Sable A lacing of black hairs over a lighter ground color.
Scent The odor left by an animal on the trail (ground scent), or wafted through the air (airborne scent).
Scissors bite A bite in which the outer side of the lower incisors touches the inner side of the upper incisors.
Tongue The barking or baying of hounds on the trail, to give tongue, to open or speak.
Whelps Unweaned puppies.
Wind To catch the scent of game.
Withers The highest point of the shoulders.

External Appearance

What differentiates the dachshund from almost any other breed of dog is its long body combined with short legs. The breed characteristics of the dachshund were set down in Germany over a hundred years ago. Of course, a number of changes were made in the course of the following decades, leading up to the standard that is now prescribed by the FCI (Fédération Cynologique Internationale), on which the official standard of the AKC is in turn based.

Official AKC Standard for the Dachshund*

*From *The Complete Dog Book*, official publication of the American Kennel Club, 16th edition, 1983.

General Appearance: Low to ground, short-legged, long-bodied, but with compact figure and robust development; with bold and confident carriage of the head and intelligent facial expression. In spite of his shortness of leg, in comparison with his length of trunk, he should appear neither crippled, awkward, cramped in his capacity for movement, nor slim and weasel-like.

Qualities: He should be clever, lively, and courageous to the point of rashness, persevering in his work both above and below ground; with all the senses well developed. His build and disposition qualify him especially for hunting game below ground. Added to this, his hunting spirit, good nose, loud tongue, and small size, render him especially suited for beating the bush. His figure and his fine nose give him an especial advantage over most other breeds of sporting dogs for trailing.

Conformation of Body

Head: Viewed from above or from the side, it should taper uniformly to the tip of the nose, and should be clean-cut. The skull is only slightly arched, and should slope gradually without stop (the less stop the more typical) into the finely-formed slightly-arched muzzle (ram's nose). The bridge bones over the eyes should be strongly prominent. The nasal cartilage and tip of the nose are long and narrow; lips tightly stretched, well covering the lower jaw, but neither deep nor pointed; corner of the mouth not very marked. Nostrils well open. Jaws opening wide and hinged

16

well back of the eyes, with strongly developed bones and teeth.

Teeth: Powerful canine teeth should fit closely together, and the outer side of the lower incisors should tightly touch the inner side of the upper. (Scissors bite.)

Eyes: Medium size, oval, situated at the sides, with a clean, energetic, though pleasant expression; not piercing. Color, lustrous dark reddish-brown to brownish-black for all coats and colors. Wall eyes in the case of dapple dogs are not a very bad fault, but are also not desirable.

Ears: Should be set near the top of the head, and not too far forward, long but not too long, beautifully rounded, not narrow, pointed, or folded. Their carriage should be animated, and the forward edge should just touch the cheek.

Neck: Fairly long, muscular, clean-cut, not showing any dewlap on the throat, slightly arched in the nape, extending in a graceful line into the shoulders, carried proudly but not stiffly.

Front: To endure the arduous exertion underground, the front must be correspondingly muscular, compact, deep, long and broad. Forequarters in detail:

Shoulder Blade: Long, broad, obliquely and firmly placed upon the fully developed thorax, furnished with hard and plastic muscles.

Upper Arm: Of the same length as the shoulder blade, and at right angles to the latter, strong of bone and hard of muscle, lying close to the ribs, capable of free movement.

Forearm: This is short in comparison to other breeds, slightly turned inwards; supplied with hard but plastic muscles on the front and outside, with tightly stretched tendons on the inside and at the back.

Joint between forearm and foot (wrists): These are closer together than the shoulder joints, so that the front does not appear absolutely straight.

Paws: Full, broad in front, and a trifle inclined outwards; compact, with well-arched toes and tough pads.

Toes: There are five of these, though only four are in use. They should be close together, with a pronounced arch; provided on top with strong nails, and underneath with tough toe-pads. Dewclaws may be removed.

Trunk: The whole trunk should in general be long and fully muscled. The back, with sloping shoulders, and short, rigid pelvis, should lie in the straightest possible line between the withers and the very slightly arched loins, these latter being short, rigid, and broad.

Chest: The breastbone should be strong, and so prominent in front that on either side a depression (dimple) appears. When viewed from the front, the thorax should appear oval, and should extend downward to the mid-point of the forearm. The enclosing structure of ribs should appear full and oval, and when viewed from above or from the side, full-volumed, so as to allow by its ample capacity, complete development of heart and lungs. Well ribbed up, and gradually merging into the line of the abdomen. If the length is correct, and also the anatomy of the shoulder and upper arm, the front leg when viewed in profile should cover the lowest point of the breast line.

Abdomen: Slightly drawn up.

Breed Characteristics

Hindquarters: The hindquarters viewed from behind should be of completely equal width.

Croup: Long, round, full, robustly muscled, but plastic, only slightly sinking toward the tail.

Pelvic Bones: Not too short, rather strongly developed, and moderately sloping.

Thigh Bone: Robust and of good length, set at right angles to the pelvic bones.

Hind Legs: Robust and well-muscled, with well-rounded buttocks.

Knee Joint: Broad and strong.

Calf Bone: In comparison with other breeds, short; it should be perpendicular to the thigh bone, and firmly muscled.

The bones at the base of the foot (tarsus) should present a flat appearance, with a strongly prominent hock and a broad tendon of Achilles.

The central foot bones (metatarsus): should be long, movable toward the calf bone, slightly bent toward the front, but perpendicular (as viewed from behind).

Hind Paws: Four compactly closed and beautifully arched toes, as in the case of the front paws. The whole foot should be posed equally on the ball and not merely on the toes; nails short.

Tail: Set in continuation of the spine, extending without any pronounced curvature, and should not be carried too gaily. *Note—Inasmuch as the dachshund is a hunting dog, scars from honorable wounds shall not be considered a fault.*

Special Characteristics of the Three Coat Varieties

The dachshund is bred with three varieties of coat: (1) Short-haired (or Smooth); (2) Wirehaired; (3) Long-haired. All three varieties should conform to the characteristics already specified. The long-haired and short-haired are old, well-fixed varieties, but into the wirehaired dachshund, the blood of other breeds has been purposely introduced; nevertheless, in breeding him, the greatest stress must be placed upon conformity to the general dachshund type. The following specifications are applicable separately to the three coat-varieites, respectively:

(1) Short-haired (or Smooth) Dachshund

Hair: Short, thick, smooth and shining; no bald patches. Special faults are: Too fine or thin hair, leathery ears, bald patches, too coarse or too thick hair in general.

Tail: Gradually tapered to a point, well but not too richly haired, long, sleek bristles on the underside are considered a patch of strong-growing hair, not a fault. A brush tail is a fault, as is also a partly or wholly hairless tail.

Color of Hair, Nose and Nails

One-Colored Dachshund: This group includes red (often called tan), red-yellow, yellow, and brindle, with or without a shading of interspersed black hairs. Nevertheless a clean color is preferable, and red is to be considered more desirable than red-yellow or yellow. Dogs strongly shaded with interspersed black hairs belong to this class, and not to the other color groups. A small white spot is admissable, but not desirable. Nose and Nails—black; brown is admissible, but not desirable.

Breed Characteristics

Two-Colored Dachshund: These comprise deep black, chocolate, gray (blue), and white; each with tan markings over the eyes, on the sides of the jaw and underlip, on the inner edge of the ear, front, breast, inside and behind the front legs, on the paws and around the anus, and from there to about one-third to one-half of the length of the tail on the under side. The most common two-colored dachshund is usually called black-and-tan. A small white spot is admissible but not desirable. Absence, undue prominence or extreme lightness of tan markings is undesirable. Nose and Nails—in the case of black dogs, black; for chocolate, brown (the darker the better); for gray (blue) or white dogs, gray or even flesh color, but the last named color is not desirable; in the case of white dogs, black nose and nails are to be preferred.

Dappled Dachshund: The color of the dappled dachshund is a clear brownish or grayish color, or even a white ground, with dark irregular patches of dark-gray, red-yellow or black (large areas of one color not desirable). It is desirable that neither the light nor the dark color should predominate. Nose and Nails—as for one- and two-colored dachshund.

(2) Wirehaired Dachshund

The general appearance is the same as that of the short-haired, but without being long in the legs, it is permissible for the body to be somewhat higher off the ground.

Hair: With the exception of jaw, eyebrows, and ears, the whole body is covered with perfectly uniform tight, short, thick, rough, hard coat, but with finer, shorter hairs (undercoat) everywhere distributed between the coarser hairs, resembling the coat of the German wirehaired pointer. There should be a beard on the chin. The eyebrows are bushy. On the ears the hair is shorter than on the body; almost smooth, but in any case conforming to the rest of the coat. The general arrangement of the hair should be such that the wirehaired dachshund, when seen from a distance, should resemble the smooth-haired. Any short of soft hair in the coat is faulty, whether short or long, or wherever found on the body; the same is true of long, curly, or wavy hair that sticks out irregularly in all directions; a flag tail is also objectionable.

Tail: Robust, as thickly haired as possible, gradually coming to a point, and without a tuft.

Color of Hair, Nose and Nails: All colors are admissible. White patches on the chest, though allowable, are not desirable.

(3) Long-haired Dachshund

The distinctive characteristic differentiating this coat from the short-haired, or smooth-haired dachshund is alone the rather long silky hair.

Hair: The soft, sleek, glistening, often slightly wavy hair should be longer under the neck, on the underside of the body, and especially on the ears and behind the legs, becoming there a pronounced feather; the hair should attain its greatest length on the underside of the tail. The hair should fall beyond the lower edge of the ear. Short hair on the ear, so-called "leather"

Breed Characteristics

ears, is not desirable. Too luxurious a coat causes the long-haired dachshund to seem coarse, and masks the type. The coat should remind one of the Irish setter, and should give the dog an elegant appearance. Too thick hair on the paws, so-called "mops," is inelegant, and renders the animal unfit for use. It is faulty for the dog to have equally long hair over all the body, if the coat is too curly, or too scrubby, or if a flag or overhanging hair on the ears are lacking; or if there is a very pronounced parting on the back, or a vigorous growth between the toes.

Tail: Carried gracefully in prolongation of the spine; the hair attains here its greatest length and forms a veritable flag.

Color of Hair, Nose and Nails: Exactly as for the smooth-haired dachshund, except that the red-with-black (heavily sabled) color is permissible and is formally classed as a red.

Miniature Dachshunds

Note—Miniature dachshunds are bred in all three coats. Within the limits imposed, symmetrical adherence to the general dachshund conformation, combined with smallness, and mental and physical vitality, should be the outstanding characteristics of miniature dachshunds. They have not been given separate classification but are a division of the Open Class for "under 10 pounds, and 12 months old or over."

General Faults

Serious Faults: Over- or undershot jaws, knuckling over, very loose shoulders.

Secondary Faults: A weak, long-legged, or dragging figure; body hanging between the shoulders; sluggish, clumsy, or waddling gait; toes turned inwards or too obliquely outwards; splayed paws; sunken back, roach (or carp) back; croup higher than withers; short-ribbed or too weak chest; excessively drawn-up flanks like those of a greyhound; narrow, poorly muscled hindquarters; weak loins; bad angulation in front or hindquarters; cowhocks; bowed legs; wall eyes, except for dappled dogs; bad coat.

Minor Faults: Ears wrongly set, sticking out, narrow or folded; too marked a stop; too pointed or weak a jaw; pincer teeth; too wide or too short a head; goggle eyes, wall eyes in the case of dappled dogs, insufficiently dark eyes in the case of all other coat-colors; dewlaps; short neck; swan neck; too fine or too thin hair; absence of, or too profuse or too light tan markings in the case of two-colored dogs.

For the ordinary dog owner who keeps a dachshund primarily for company, a detailed discussion of defects or flaws that might detract from a dog's value as breeding stock or cost points at a show is not of great interest. Anyone who wants a dachshund as a family dog and companion on walks is likely to base the choice on nothing more than taste and informed reflection, "Well, this is the puppy I really like."

For people who might eventually like to show their dogs or who toy with the idea of breeding dachshunds, a knowledge of the breed characteristics is important. If

Breed Characteristics

you happen to have acquired a dachshund
that—according to the standard—has severe enough flaws to rank it low in a
show, you are bound to be disappointed. If
you have hopes of ending up with a cham-
pion, you should join the Dachshund Club
of America and attend meetings of your local chapter to learn exactly what all the
specialized terms mean. When you have a
real live model to look at, it is a lot easier
to learn. You should also have the advice
of an expert when you select your puppy.
An expert may not detect every conceiv-
able flaw, but will recognize most and
probably keep you from picking a real
loser.

Housing and Equipment

Basket or Box?

Dogs have a marked sense of order. To prevent your dog from establishing its own order—which may not always conform to your wishes—you should make sure from the very beginning that it adjusts to yours. First, it needs a pleasant place of its own—a place it will seek out eventually of its own free will. Cavelike baskets are very popular; dachshunds appreciate a roof over their heads. With a young puppy, however, the basket often does not remain whole for long. The wickerwork is all too tempting for testing young teeth on. That is why you may prefer at first to set up a carton or box of appropriate size with an opening cut in

Dachshunds are fond of dragging the family clothes or shoes to their beds.

the front. Later on, whether you pick a carton or a basket is up to your pocketbook.

A Suitable Sleeping Place

The bed—whether box or basket—should be located in the right place, which means a quiet, draft-free corner. The dog should have a good view of everything, so it can watch what is happening and feel part of the household. This helps it learn quite a bit, too. At the same time it should feel that it has some privacy. A young dog needs a lot of sleep. If its bed is right next to a "traffic lane," the noise and its own curiosity keep rousing it. It will also continually be tempted to leave the bed. That is why it is in your interest and the dog's to give some careful thought at the beginning to where the dog should sleep and to find as ideal a solution as possible.

Basic Equipment

The most important items should be all set up when the new member of the household arrives—that is, a food dish, a water bowl, a box or basket lined with a blanket, and a collar and leash. This "basic equipment" must be chosen with care.

The food dish must be heavy enough so that it is not pushed all over the floor when the dog is eating. Enameled dishes with a rubber strip around the bottom edge to prevent sliding are very practical. These dishes are more expensive than plastic but they are worth the price because they last for years.

24

Housing and Equipment

Collars do not last for years; a young dog outgrows its first collar within a few months. That is why a plain thin leather collar is quite adequate for a puppy. The first leash also can be of plain leather. Almost all puppies and young dogs chew the lower end of their leashes in an attempt to get free. Some leashes have a short piece of chain at the lower end. However, there is some debate on the advisability of such leashes, since chewing on the hard metal links may not be good for the puppy's teeth.

A fully grown dachshund needs a more sturdy collar and a regular leash for walking as well as an extra long one. In addition to the long leather leashes used for training dogs, there are also leashes made of synthetic materials with automatic take-up devices.

For some special situations—travel abroad and visits to the veterinarian, for instance—a muzzle may also be necessary.

A brush should also be included in the basic equipment. Your little dachshund should get used right away to a daily brushing. It feels good and is healthy. For a long-haired or a wirehaired dachshund, a brush that also has wire bristles on one side is appropriate. A short-haired dachshund needs only a brush with natural (rather than nylon) bristles.

A louse comb—that is, a comb with very fine, narrow teeth—should also be included. Even the best-tended dog occasionally gets fleas. All it has to do is get close to an infested dog. If your dog keeps scratching, a louse comb will quickly show whether lice are the cause.

And finally, you need clippers to trim your dog's toenails if they do not get worn down sufficiently by running.

The Right Toys

Let us not forget toys. They have a very important function for a young dog that wants and needs to use its teeth. There are squeaky toys that can drive both owner and dog crazy—the dog because the squeaking gets it excited which keeps it chewing harder and harder with all the more squeaking. In addition, some dogs manage very quickly to take the thing apart, and they may then swallow the metal "squeaker." If this small object does not soon pass through the digestive system naturally, surgery may become necessary to remove it.

Plastic toys are dangerous because they usually come in shapes that make it easy for a dog to bite off and swallow pieces. That is why I have always preferred balls and rings made of solid rubber. A dog can chew on them to its heart's content; they are remarkably resistant to sharp little teeth and are unlikely to cause any harm. Hollow objects are always dangerous. They can usually be destroyed too easily and the pieces swallowed. Toys made of wood are especially dangerous because of splinters.

The popular toys made of rawhide are quite useful, but some caution is in order. One of my dachshunds once almost choked to death on a piece of rawhide that he had bitten off and that was just a little too large. He tried to swallow it, and it literally got stuck in his throat. Luckily I noticed it and was able to remove it. If I had not happened to be in the same room, I might have found a dead dog on my return.

Some people recommend giving a young dog an old shoe to play with. This is not a good idea. How is a dog to know the difference between an old shoe and the shoes you still want to wear? It is quite annoying to find your dog has been exercising its teeth on your newest pair.

The same problems arise with paper, of whatever kind. The dog cannot tell the difference between today's paper and yester-

day's, nor does it have any way of knowing whether the piece of paper it finds on the hall floor is a letter the mailman has just delivered or some meaningless scrap.

It is *you* who must be aware of all these possibilities. A dog, especially a young puppy, cannot be.

A little dachshund learns its first lessons through play. It is essential to stick to the same word for any one command.

Basic Rules of Dachshund Care

Getting the Puppy Settled

A new life begins for a puppy when you take it home and it has to get used to your way of life.

It is a satisfying task, but not an easy one, to help your new dog adjust to the great change. The first problem that comes up is loneliness. A puppy that has been used to being close to its mother and siblings all the time, both awake and asleep, now finds itself alone in a basket or box and is expected to spend the whole night there. This is hard, but the dog will simply have to learn to cope with this situation, and the sooner it does, the better. This is a lot to expect of an animal that nature intended to live in a pack, and only a few dogs submit to this fate without more or less vociferous protest. For your part, you will find that it takes all the sympathy and patience you can muster.

Gentle and Harsh Methods

You can choose between a gentle and a harsh approach for teaching your puppy to adjust to its new life. If you opt for gentleness, you can place its bed next to yours so that the little transplant at least feels another creature nearby. Then, if it starts to complain you can console it with some petting and reassuring words.

The disadvantage of this method is that the dog is not really forced to change its habits; it is not learning to be by itself. It may keep quiet at night, but it will object all the more loudly if you leave it alone during the day. I know quite a few dog owners who do not dare to leave the house and have to get a "dog sitter" if they want to go out at night because the dachshund will keep the whole neighborhood awake with its howling.

If you decide on the harsh method, you move the basket into a room where your dachshund cannot cause any damage. The kitchen or bathroom is best. Then you leave it alone. Only if it gets very noisy should you go to see it briefly, tell it firmly to lie on its bed, and pet it a little to calm it down. Most dogs make their peace with the new situation quickly and give up their howls of protest. I admit that this procedure sounds rather heartless. It has one great advantage, however: a dog that learns right away that there are times when it has to be alone will also be able to spend longer periods—several hours at a stretch—by itself without barking, and it will have to learn this sooner or later if you are not going to become its slave. This is why I think it is better to teach the lesson right away. The only complication that may arise is if you live in an apartment house with poor sound-proofing. Keep in mind that your dog will have to learn to cope with solitude sooner or later and that the decibel level of its protest will increase with its age. I would therefore advise you to pay your neighbors a visit—including those living immediately above and below—to explain the situation and ask them to put up with a few nights (it rarely takes longer) of dog noises.

◁ Above: Long-haired dachshund puppies, six weeks old. Below: Long-haired dachshund mother nursing her litter.

Basic Rules of Dachshund Care

Staying Alone—The "Security" Room

If the gentle method is more in your line or if thin walls and uncooperative neighbors preclude the harsher procedure, you will have to resort to a different way of teaching your dog to be alone. Place it—along with its bed and a toy—in a special "security" room now and then for a while during the day.

Now, what is a security room?

A young dog, just like a human child, has an innate need to play. It does not matter in the least what it happens to find as a toy; the main thing is that it finds an object to play with. Unfortunately, our opinions in this matter rarely coincide with the dog's, and we find it not the least bit amusing if we come upon our little dachshund shredding shoes, pulling clothes from a closet, chewing on towels, or gleefully testing the durability of our living room rug. The puppy may relieve itself occasionally, too, of course, which is perfectly understandable if it is left alone for a long period of time. That is why it should be left alone in a room where it cannot get into trouble and where nobody gets upset if it leaves a little puddle. This is usually the kitchen or a bathroom without carpeting.

If the dog starts to whine and complain when placed in the "security room," scold it and tell it to lie in its basket, or refrain from responding altogether. Start with a fifteen-minute period or, if it keeps quiet, longer. Be sure to go get it again when it is really quiet and not when it is making noise. Otherwise, what it learns is, "If I just complain loudly enough they will come to get me."

Grooming Tasks

Since dachshunds—even long-haired dachshunds—do not need to be clipped or trimmed, their coat care is relatively simple and hardly costs anything. You can perform almost all the grooming tasks yourself.

Coat Care—Pests and Burrs

Grooming is obviously easiest with a short-haired (smooth) dachshund. All you have to do is brush it as regularly as possible. You can also rub it down with a cloth so that its fur lies smoothly and shines. You should have a dust or louse comb

If your dachshund was purchased primarily as a playmate for your child, the child should take over some of the responsibility for daily care.

Basic Rules of Dachshund Care

(page 25) in case it does catch fleas at some point. Louse combs work quite well for getting rid of fleas, but you have to watch that these pests do not simply jump off their host. To kill them I dip the comb in Dermaton, Paramite, or Kem Dip both before and after using it. If combing fails to control the pests, add Dermaton, Paramite, Kem Dip, or Para Dip to a small, plastic tub of water, place the dog inside, and then rinse the dog thoroughly with lukewarm water without using any shampoo.

External parasite infestations can also be effectively combated with the aid of appropriate powders and sprays. Always make sure to use them in strict conformity to the instructions. Too big a dosage can have severe consequences. Dogs that have been dusted with the powder should, if at all possible, not get wet. Otherwise, skin irritations can result. Some dogs are allergic to sprays, just like people. That is why I always prefer to use the comb alone, though it may appear rather "primitive" in comparison with insecticides and flea collars.

Ticks must be treated with alcohol or a special liquid first and removed with tweezers. Failure to remove the tick's head can cause infection.

Long-haired and wirehaired dachshunds take a little more time to groom. They not only have to be "worked over" with a brush but also need to be groomed with a comb or a brush that has wire bristles. Be sensitive, careful, and gentle when applying the wire bristles; they should never be allowed to scratch. Dachshunds are sensitive, and they do not like it even if "it

pulls," let alone scratches the skin.

Outside of the city, plants can cause dachshunds to return home covered with seeds of all sorts, especially in summer. The ears get the worst, and there is the danger that the seeds will work their way up into the ear canal and cause inflammation (pages 32, 44). It is advisable, therefore, to remove these annoying foreign objects as soon as possible. Use a fine-toothed comb, and check the inside of the cial care.

Burrs are also a great nuisance. They can get so matted into the hair on the chest, abdomen, and legs that the dog is reluctant to go on. It is not all that easy to remove them, either. Once I had to carry a dachshund for several hundred yards because he refused to walk and I was unable to remove the mass of burrs. Since that time I always take a small pair of scissors along with me. You should also watch that your dachshund does not try to pull the burrs out of its own hair. My female dachshund once got a burr stuck in her throat this way. This was not only unpleasant but dangerous. Her esophagus did not get really cleaned out until I got her to swallow some mashed potato. You are safest if you remove all burrs from your dog's coat as promptly as possible.

Teeth and Nails

Grooming also includes checking the dog's teeth and nails. Toenails that are too long can be a hindrance in running and cause painful changes in the posture of the paws. That is why you should trim overgrown nails from time to time with claw

Basic Rules of Dachshund Care

clippers. You should proceed with caution not to injure the quick—the flesh underneath the nail. If you are unsure about trying this yourself, the veterinarian can do it for you.

The teeth should be checked for plaque. If there is just a little, the veterinarian can scratch it off quickly, but if there is a buildup of plaque, it must be removed under anesthesia with an ultrasonic device.

Ears

Watch your dog to make sure that it does not keep scratching its ears. This could be a sign of an ear infection. This disorder, which should be treated by a veterinarian if it occurs, can be largely prevented if you take good and regular care of your dog's ears by cleaning them carefully once a week with a dry cotton swab.

Baths

What about baths? I am not in favor of unnecessary bathing. If we have gone for a walk in bad weather and the dogs come home with their legs and bellies covered with mud, I stand them in a plastic tub and rinse them off with lukewarm water (no shampoo). Then they are rubbed dry or, if they have gotten too wet, blown dry. I never bathe my dogs just to enhance their beauty, since regular brushing keeps them perfectly clean.

For a city dog this simple way of staying clean is not quite sufficient. Although the dirt in the countryside is usually still "natural"—that is, it is simply wet earth—dogs that live in the city are exposed to all the blessings of our civilization, such as exhaust fumes, smoke, dust, and chemicals. Under these conditions it may become necessary from time to time to give a dog a real shampoo bath, but please be sure to use a special dog shampoo, and above all, do not give too many. The more a dog is bathed, the softer and less dirt-resistant its hair becomes because it loses its waterproof quality (a dog's skin and hair are naturally protected). Bathe your dog if necessary, but do not overdo it. All grooming should be done in moderation and preferably by the dog's owner, not at a dog grooming parlor.

Traveling with Your Dachshund

You can take your dog almost anywhere in the world, except for a few countries with quarantine regulations, such as Great Britain, Sweden, and Norway. It can travel with you by air, train, or boat, and you can of course take it in your car. When you plan your vacation you should also give some thought to your dog and ask yourself whether the strain of a long trip might not be too much for it. Ask at the appropriate office (railway, shipping company, or airline) or your travel agent about regulations concerning pet travel. Find out in plenty of time, too, what rules for the entry of animals apply in the country you wish to visit. Consulates and automobile associations have this information available.

Motion Sickness

Motion sickness causes the fewest prob-

Basic Rules of Dachshund Care

lems if you take your dog along in your own car, but even here some difficulties are likely. Dachshunds tend to get carsick and often begin to vomit after they have been riding in a car for a while. Find out ahead of time how your dog reacts to car travel. This can save you a lot of trouble. If necessary, your veterinarian can prescribe medication against motion sickness. Try first to get your dog used to riding in a car. I have done this successfully a number of times, but it takes two people with enough time and patience, the driver and another person. It is also useful to drive along quiet streets so that you can pull over to the side quickly if necessary. The nondriver must watch the dog carefully because a dog almost always indicates when it is about to get sick. Increased panting, nervous licking, and general restlessness mean, stop. You get out of the car with the dog on a leash, walk up and down with it for a while, letting it sniff and perhaps relieve itself. In a short while the dog is distracted, fills its lungs with fresh oxygen, and feels considerably better.

You have to go through this routine more than once. Puppies are particularly subject to motion sickness. For them riding in a car is an altogether unnatural experience.

Necessary Precautions

Once your dog has gotten used to riding in a car, you can take it along on longer trips, but make sure you take plenty of water for it. You never know how hot it is going to be or how long you might be stuck in a traffic jam. Your dog could die if you don't have any water to give it in such a situation.

When you park your car (in the shade) and leave your dachshund, look to see where the sun is and always leave a window partially open, or you might come back to find your poor dog very ill or even expired.

Do not let your dog stick its head out of an open window while the car is moving. Severe inflammation of the eyes and ears, as well as bad colds, can result.

When you stop at a rest area, always put a leash on the dog before getting out of the car. More than one poor dachshund, happy

This is a poor and dangerous practice. Dogs can catch colds if they ride with their heads out of windows.

Basic Rules of Dachshund Care

to get out of this box on wheels, has run straight under the wheels of another car.

Do not overfeed your dog before or during the trip; there is no fear of its starving. And do make sure that it always has plenty of water.

First-Aid Kit for Travel

If you take along a few items for your dog in your first-aid kit, you can set out on a trip without fear of disaster. I would advise you to include the following: Kaopectate, Paregoric, or Lomotil (for diarrhea), mineral oil or milk of magnesia (for constipation), some powder or a spray against parasites, bandages and a healing salve for which you may need a prescription from your veterinarian.

Dachshunds and Children

Are dachshunds fond of children? This question cannot be answered with a simple yes or no. There is no breed of dog that "loves children," just as there is none that by nature detests them. There are individual dogs of certain breeds that I would hesitate to recommend for a family with children, especially very young ones. The dachshund certainly does not number among these.

A dog's personal disposition is only a minor element in whether it will develop into a friend of children or the opposite. Much more important are the experiences it has with children. If a dog of any breed is continually teased and tormented by children, it is most unlikely to harbor friendly

feelings toward them. On the contrary, it will see in every child a potential tormenter, will try to avoid being touched, and will growl or bite instead. Should we blame and scold it for that? After all, it is not the dog's fault that it developed this way.

There are among dachshunds some less gregarious types that reserve their affections exclusively for their master or mistress. They would never harm anybody, but they like to be left in peace. These

A dog is a playmate, not a toy. This is something you must teach your children right away.

dogs are not ideal candidates for families with children. You can already recognize this type of personality in a puppy. If you have children, choose a cheerful, outgoing little puppy that approaches you and your

34

children eagerly. Then you are unlikely to have any difficulties.

Explain to your children until they really understand that a dog is not a toy but a lovable companion that needs to have its rest now and then and does not like to be dragged around all the time. It happens

Never lift a dachshund up by the scruff of its neck. To pick it up properly, reach one hand around the dog's rib cage, and support its rear with the other hand.

sometimes that a child gets scratched when romping around with a dachshund, and some dogs snap lightly in play. The teeth, particularly the sharp little baby teeth, can inflict quite painful bites. All this should have no great dampening effect on the friendship between child and dog. Children

usually love their four-legged friends with great devotion.

What is the story if a couple with a dachshund is expecting a baby? Dogs can indeed become jealous if they—who up to now were the center of attention—are suddenly relegated to the sidelines and practically ignored. Don't let this happen and the baby will very quickly be accepted by the dog as a new member of the family. A friendship will come into being that will last for the length of the dog's life.

Raising Dachshunds

Estrus (Heat) and What to Do About It

Male dogs become sexually mature at about one year old. Female dogs, called bitches, become sexually receptive for the first time at about seven to nine months old. After that females become sexually receptive every six to ten months. The estrus or "heat" period, as this time is generally called, lasts about three weeks. Restlessness and increased appetite announce its onset. There is an easy way to prevent your dog from leaving bloodstains in the house: put a pair of special diaperlike panties on her while she is indoors. They are available in most better pet stores or obtainable through your veterinarian. Needless to say, the "heat" period brings some other problems for the dog's owner (pages 12–13).

You should let your dog go through a normal heat twice before you take steps to prevent it either by spaying or hormone injections. In addition, most veterinarians advise that these injections be discontinued or at least interrupted after two or three sessions to allow the dog to undergo a normal heat again and let the normal body functions resume.

Pregnancy and Whelping

Many owners of female dachshunds have a desire to breed their dogs, but there are certain conditions that should be met. Anyone wishing to breed dachshunds should have extensive experience in keeping dogs; he or she should also be a member of the Dachshund Club of America and be familiar with the literature on breeding dachshunds, which the club will supply. The minimum age at which dogs are officially allowed to be bred—this applies to males as well as females—is one year, although I prefer for the female to wait until her third heat. After mating takes place, a litter can be expected in about 63 days or about two months.

During pregnancy it is particularly important to give your dog food rich in vitamins supplemented with calcium tablets and to make sure she gets enough exercise, without overexertion.

When your female dachshund is in heat, you may have to put up with an obtrusive crowd of admirers.

Raising Dachshunds

You should start to make preparations for the whelping, or birth, well ahead of the expected due date. A whelping box (available at pet stores) should be placed in a warm, draft-free, out-of-the-way spot. If you do not wish to purchase a whelping box, you may use several layers of newspapers covered with soft clean cloths.

As whelping time approaches, the bitch becomes restless and refuses to eat. Her teats become swollen and often secrete a little milk. Early labor pains gradually increase into regular contractions. After approximately one to three hours of labor, the water breaks and the first puppy arrives. After that, at intervals of about fifteen minutes, the rest of the litter follows. There may be six or more puppies in a typical litter.

The mother breaks the amniotic sac surrounding each puppy, bites off the umbilical cord, and licks the newborn puppy until it starts breathing. The puppy then usually begins to nurse.

You should be prepared to call the veterinarian if any trouble seems to be developing. Unpleasant complications can arise even when you know all you think there is to know and after you have taken the most meticulous precautions, as I found out to my distress.

Sixteen days after giving birth to three puppies, my dachshund was lying in her basket obviously very sick. She was suddenly seized by convulsions, and it was clearly a matter of life or death. A few minutes after the veterinarian, whom I had contacted immediately, had given her a calcium gluconate injection intravenously for her heart, the cramps began to subside. What had happened?

"Nursing toxemia," milk fever, puerperal tetany, or eclampsia is what this condition is called. Only bitches that are good nursing mothers are affected by it. It seems that the calcium balance of the body becomes upset, manifesting itself in severe convulsions accompanied by breathing difficulties that can lead to heart failure if help comes too late. The situation can recur, and utmost vigilance is therefore in order.

In addition to eclampsia other problems can arise during whelping. Especially among small breeds, complications in giving birth are unfortunately rather common. Dachshunds have neither overly large heads—a condition that frequently necessitates Caesarian surgery in some breeds—nor any other abnormal physical shapes. Small dogs generally have small litters, however, and the fewer puppies there are in a litter, the larger the individual animals tend to be, which can make for a difficult birth. Be sure, therefore, never to leave your dog alone at whelping time. It is not only nonsense but also sheer irresponsibility to claim that a dog prefers to give birth alone and feels human presence to be an intrusion of privacy.

Training Starts Early

After the pups are born, take the time to watch the mother teach her young the skills they need for life. She will play with her babies, using play to teach appropriate behavior, but she will also insist on rules as

Raising Dachshunds

the babies grow, and she will resort to physical punishment if the young misbehave. There is no way of getting around it: anyone who lives in a community with others must learn to fit in. This also applies to dogs, which naturally live in packs. When we pick up our little puppy at just a few weeks old, we are understandably charmed by this cute little creature that snuggles in our arms seeking protection. "You cannot start training such a helpless, innocent little puppy," you may think. The younger a dog is, the more receptive it is; it learns easily and adjusts quickly. That is why you should initiate training early—within limits, of course.

The first thing to clarify is who will be the primary teacher. In most cases this role will devolve on the person who spends the most time at home. It is important that everybody in the family use the same words when teaching the dog so that it hears identical commands from all the members of the household. It is a rewarding task to raise a young dog and train it properly, but it takes time—lots of time (page 58).

Rules for Breeding Dachshunds

The primary requisites for permission to breed a dog are good health, strong development, and absolute conformity to the breed's physical traits.

A dachshund that is going to be bred should have a powerful and muscular body. Dogs that look soft and flabby and timid animals are not accepted as breeding stock. A dachshund cannot be used for breeding until it is one year old, and it obviously cannot have any congenital defects. Apart from these basic rules there are detailed regulations that apply to the entry of dogs in the registry of the Dachshund Club of America. The registry is open to any dachshund breeder, assuming that he or she recognizes and follows the regulations of the club.

Any dachshund bred in the United States is eligible for entry to the AKC. Proof must be submitted that the dog is a purebred dachshund, and the animal must be vaccinated against canine distemper and in-

Anyone considering raising dachshunds should be aware that this enterprise requires lots of time and effort.

fectious canine hepatitis. A dog imported from abroad is accepted only if its pedigree is vouched for by the registry office of the FCI (Fédération Cynologique Internationale) responsible for the geographic area in question.

Offspring of dachshunds imported from abroad are entered in the AKC registry only if the pedigrees of one or both parents are vouched for by a registry office abroad that is associated with the FCI.

Excluded from entry in the registry are dachshunds that
• are the result of crossing strains of different coat textures
• have no valid pedigrees
• come from kennels that have been rejected by the AKC registry
• have been bought and sold by dealers.

These are some of the main points covered by the regulations. Any further information you might want—if you are considering breeding your dog—can be obtained by writing to the AKC or DCA (page 70).

The Proper Diet

Some General Remarks

No aspect of how to keep and care for a dog has undergone as radical a change in the last couple of decades as the question of what dogs should eat. Dogs used to be, and still are, given all kinds of food, ranging from the obvious to the most unlikely. These dogs stay alive, but they are probably not very healthy. I know of a German shepherd that was given practically nothing but bones—and not the best bones by far—that lived to a ripe old age, though I would hate to think what his state of health really was. Some people I know feed their dogs exclusively on table scraps. The dogs are given all the leftovers, including rich sauces and gravies, hot spices, and everything else that does not agree with canine digestive systems. These animals, too, survive without apparent major damage to their health.

Such methods of feeding are obviously not to be recommended. A proper diet is much better for our dogs, but just what constitutes a proper diet?

Home-Prepared or Commercial Food?

Some people swear that the traditional way of feeding a dog—that is, fresh meat and grain products—is the best. Others have been converted to commercial dog food. The traditionalists are skeptical about the virtues of commercial food, but those who use it point out that their dogs are hale and healthy, and they see no reason to change their ways. Since I have run into so many people who expressed doubts about the claims made for commercial dog food in advertisements, I decided to take part in a tour of one of the major animal food companies. What I saw at this plant removed whatever doubts I might have had. The food is composed individually for different kinds of animals—including dogs, obviously—in accordance with up-to-date research on nutrition. The cans and packages actually contain everything that is listed on their labels.

Therefore, anyone wanting to make sure their dog gets an absolutely correct diet should choose commercial food, but I would urge all those who are still opposed to commercial food to at least get their dogs used to it for convenience. If you travel with your dog, it may be difficult to prepare your own food or to find healthy food on the trip or buy it wherever you are.

Whether you prepare your dog's food yourself or buy commercial dog food, the important thing is that it get all the essential nutrients.

The Proper Diet

Types of Commercial Dog Food

What is the composition of commercial dog food, and what kinds are there? Taking into account the eating habits of dogs and what appeals to them, companies produce four basic types of dog food.

Canned dog food contains all the nutrients necessary for a dog. It is made up of meats (such as muscle meat, tripe, heart, liver, and lung), grains (such as rice, barley, oats, wheat, or corn), and added vitamins and minerals.

Since dogs can utilize carbohydrates even though they are basically meat eaters, manufacturers produce two kinds of canned dog food. One kind is a mixture of meat and carbohydrates, and the other consists primarily of meat and other sources of protein. This latter type can be mixed with up to a third of cooked potatoes, rice or grains.

Dry and semidry dog food has basically the same nutritional composition as canned dog food. The main difference is that in the former the water content has been reduced to as little as 10 or 20 percent. In canned dog food, the natural moisture content of the meat and grain products make up about 75 percent. Dry and semidry dog food is thus considerably more concentrated. A dog eating this type of food has to make up for this lack of moisture by drinking more water.

Semimoist dog food is also nutritionally complete. Its moisture content—about 25 percent—lies between that of dry and canned dog food. In other words, semimoist dog food is also considerably more

concentrated than canned dog food. The dog's need for fluids is only partially satisfied by the moisture in the food, and water must be supplied to provide the rest.

Amount of Food

Usually the label on the product will attempt to indicate how much food you should give to your dachshund, but do not follow the directions slavishly because these directions are nothing more than guidelines. It is impossible to give any binding rules about how much a dog of a certain breed should eat. Too many factors are involved. One dog utilizes what it eats well—it quickly puts on a layer of fat—and another can eat all it wants or can get and still stays thin as a rail. One dog gets lots of exercise and therefore needs plenty of food, but another has to make do with few or short walks and should therefore be fed a far skimpier diet. Watch your dachshund: its ribs should not show, but neither should it be getting fat.

There is a big difference in food need between a growing dog and a fully grown one. Puppies and young dogs need about twice as much food in relation to their size as adult dogs. The rule I have always followed is this: young dogs are served a plentiful meal, and whatever is not eaten after ten minutes is removed. Of course, puppies should be fed considerably more often than grown dogs, who need only one meal a day. A ten- to twelve-week-old puppy should be fed five times a day—and at first at exactly the times the kennel owner from whom you purchased it indicates. A drastic change in schedule at this

The Proper Diet

age can lead to serious digestive problems. The puppy itself will let you know through a drop in appetite when it is time to shift from five to four, and later to three meals a day.

So, you will gradually reduce the number of meals a day to four, then three, and then two. By the time your dachshund is one year old, all it needs is one full meal a day. You can give this meal to it at noon or at dinner time. My dogs, for instance, get their meal at noon, but I also give them two or three small dog biscuits in the morning and again at night.

Here is one final and very important piece of advice: never feed your dog raw pork, not even the tiniest amount. Pigs can get a virus that is harmless to humans but that can be transmitted by them to other mammals. In dogs, this virus causes a disease that appears without warning and is deadly, Aujeszky's disease. Any dog that is infected with this virus dies within twenty-four to thirty-six hours. Well-cooked pork is harmless.

You will be able to tell whether you are feeding your dachshund properly by the way it looks. If it looks at you with clear and bright eyes and is not too heavy, you can feel pretty sure that it is getting what it needs. Still, you should check with the veterinarian from time to time to have your assessment confirmed.

If you give your dachshund tidbits from the table, you should not be surprised if it ends up being chubby.

If Your Dachshund Gets Sick

When a dog gets sick, it should be taken to a veterinarian promptly because only a professional can tell what is wrong. A delay can be disastrous. Do not pay attention to other dog owners who might advise you that their dog once had the same thing and to give a particular medication. If you waste time following such advice, the point of effective treatment may pass. I would rather make ten trips to the vet "too early" than be too late once.

This does not mean, however, that you should take your dog in every time it vomits or has a bout of diarrhea.

If you are a novice dog owner, you may be unsure about how to interpret possible signs of trouble, and you should not hesitate to call the veterinarian even if it might turn out to have been unnecessary. This is better than having to say in retrospect, "If only I had . . . ."

By the way, never consider giving your dog medications you have on hand for yourself or for your family. There are substances that are appropriate for curing human ills but that do not work for similar conditions in dogs. *Any* medication, no matter how "harmless," should be specially prescribed for your dog with the particular dosage indicated.

Signs of Illness

There are several signs that usually indicate that a dog is ill. Among these are changes in the coat, persistent scratching, dragging the rear, and fever.

Coat Changes and Scratching

Always pay special attention to the consistency of your dog's coat. A dog's hair tells us a lot about its state of health. A dull coat or an unnaturally shaggy look, bald spots, and excessive shedding outside the normal shedding seasons (before and after the cold season) are warning signs. If your dog scratches persistently and you are sure it is free of parasites, such as fleas, ticks, and—more rarely—lice, you have to conclude that something is wrong. The possibilities range from eczema, which causes itching, to general allergic reactions or even internal diseases like diabetes.

If your dachshund is scratching its ears a lot and shaking its head, perhaps making squeaking noises as it does so, take it to the verterinarian promptly. It may be suf-

If your dachshund scratches its ears a lot, you should make an appointment with the veterinarian.

43

Above (left): Dark short-haired dachshunds; (right): ▷
Dark long-haired dachshunds
Below: Wirehaired, short-haired, and long-haired
dachshunds posing together.

fering from an ear infection, which should not be taken lightly. An inflammation of the ear canal (external otitis) can be caused by mites or by plant seeds, especially grass seeds, that have entered the ear.

Dragging the Rear

Dragging the rear along the ground is often considered a typical sign of worm infestation. It can, in fact, signal the presence of worms, but it is much more often a sign that the dog's anal glands are not functioning properly. Have the vet check if the anal glands are clogged. If the first signs of such clogging are ignored, painful inflammation and abscesses can follow. Some dogs tend to have trouble with their anal glands.

Fever

You should be able to take your dog's temperature yourself because a fever, as well as an abnormally low temperature, is a sure sign of serious illness. Get an unbreakable thermometer for dogs from your veterinarian. When you take your dachshund's temperature, one person should hold the dog to calm it while the second person gently inserts the thermometer, which has been smeared with some lubricant, into the dog's rectum. When you do this, raise the dog's tail a little and then hold on to it together with the thermometer. This way the dog cannot interfere with the procedure by wagging its tail. Leave the thermometer in, holding it gently, for about three minutes.

What is the normal body temperature of a dog? It is slightly higher than that of humans, lying between 98.6° and 102.2°F (37° and 39°C). The temperature of young dogs is around 100.4°F (38°C); that of older dogs a little lower, between 98.6° and 100.4°F (37° and 38°C). If the temperature rises above 102.2°F (39°C)—in older dogs if it even approaches this mark—this is considered a fever. If the temperature drops below 98.6°F (37°C), this, too, is a bad sign. In both cases you should get in touch with your veterinarian right away.

Types of Illnesses

There are many illnesses that may affect a dog. Vomiting and diarrhea may be signs of a serious illness or may be relatively minor disorders relating to overeating, incorrect diet, or other factors. Worm infestation is very common, especially in puppies, and several serious infectious diseases may affect your dog. In addition, dachshunds, in particular, are subject to back problems and paralysis.

Vomiting

Vomiting is often quite normal in dogs. If you feed your dachshund bones, indigestible bits of bone may stay in the stomach and later be regurgitated. Here the rule of thumb is, if a dog throws up once or twice and then behaves normally again, there is probably nothing to worry about. If the vomiting persists or resumes, however, this is a dangerous symptom. The dog may have swallowed some object that has to be

44

removed as quickly as possible. Poisoning also manifests itself first through vomiting and diarrhea. Here, too, prompt attention is crucial.

Diarrhea

Diarrhea is often the consequence of incorrect diet. Perhaps your dog has been given too much liver. Milk, which a grown dog does not need but sometimes gets, often acts as a laxative, or maybe your dog has simply had water that was too cold. In a case like this all you have to do is cut back on its food, giving it only some cooked cereal like oatmeal and dry biscuits. If it is still suffering from diarrhea the next day, then you should take it in. Prolonged diarrhea not only weakens the animal but can also be a sign of a serious disease.

Internal Parasites—Worms

A common condition dogs suffer from very frequently is worm infestation. Puppies almost inevitably have roundworms. A conscientious kennel keeper administers the first deworming to the puppies before they leave, but this treatment must be repeated. When you take your puppy to the veterinarian for its shots, you should take along a fresh stool sample to be tested for the presence of endoparasites. Tapeworms are not as widespread in dogs as roundworms, but they must be combated immediately with prescribed cures. Dogs also get hookworms, threadworms, and whipworms. These parasites occur primarily in animals raised in badly kept kennels. Since any de-

worming weakens the animal somewhat, I should like to emphasize once more, let your veterinarian determine the proper medication and follow-up treatment.

Paralysis

Because of its "unnatural" proportions, long back and short legs, dachshunds' spinal cords are subject to greater than usual stress. This can in some cases lead to slipped or ruptured disks especially in dogs over seven. Depending on the place in the spine where this occurs and on the seriousness of the case, a quick recovery may be possible. Occasionally, though, paralysis of the hindquarters results. Sometimes this can be cured, but unfortunately only rarely. And even then, recurrence is quite frequent. How quickly the patient receives treatment is often crucial.

You should take your dachshund to be examined at the slightest sign of back trouble. Perhaps your dog has jumped off a chair, yelped, walked somewhat stiffly for a while, and then everything seemed fine. This is a clear sign that the dog is a likely candidate for a slipped disk, and it would be a good idea to discuss this matter with your veterinarian. (Also, make sure that your dog does not jump off chairs anymore.) Recent discoveries in veterinary medicine make a cure of this serious condition with its potentially crippling consequences possible.

Since the symptoms are not always clear and ailments sometimes vanish as suddenly as they appear, here are some warning signs:
• Stiff posture;

47

- Over-sensitivity or apparent pain in the areas of the thoracic or lumbar vertebrae;
- Abnormal reluctance to move;
- Abnormal movements.

Veterinarians distinguish between two progressive phases in the course of the disease: the painful stage and the crippling stage. Treatment with medications is effective in about half the cases, but even then more serious relapses are likely. Surgery offers a much brighter picture, but it must be performed by a specialist. If at all possible, the operation should be performed at the painful stage and not later. Three to four days after the surgery, the patient is free of pain, and it can be taken home after ten days of treatment.

If a dachshund is suddenly afflicted with partial paralysis—that is, if it is no longer able to walk—the operation should be performed within six to twenty-four hours. Any longer delay lessens the chance of cure. As long as the paralysis has not yet affected the bladder, a successful operation is still possible even after four to five days. The convalescence period after surgery at this stage lasts three weeks·on the average. If the surgery is undertaken at a later stage, the outlook is clearly less good: recovery may take up to three months, if it comes at all.

Paralysis is much rarer when it is the thoracic (chest) vertebrae that are injured. Usually only the right or the left front leg is affected, though the condition is very painful. In these cases, the veterinarian will usually try first to bring relief through an extended course of treatment with medications. If this does not lead to improvement, an operation will follow sooner or

later, depending on the severity of the pain. The incidence of relapses after successful surgery is only about 2 percent.

It is interesting to note that in 1971 the committee of the DCA sponsored a Disk Disease Seminar in Detroit, resulting in a fund-raising program. The money—contributed by DCA regional dachshund clubs and all-breed clubs, among others—goes to the Small Animal Clinic at Auburn University in Auburn, Alabama, where a dedicated staff, under the direct supervision of Dr. B. F. Hoerlein, a distinguished veterinarian, conducts research on every issue pertaining to intervertebral disk disease.

Infectious Diseases

Among the most serious infectious diseases of dachshunds are distemper, canine hepatitis, leptospirosis, and rabies.

Distemper

This dangerous infectious disease has lost much of its terror since the advent of an effective vaccine. The first signs of this disease are fever, a runny nose, teary eyes, and diarrhea. Of course, any dog may sometimes get a harmless cold that also makes its nose run and eyes tear. Do take note of these symptoms, however, and watch your dog carefully. If its distemper vaccinations are up to date, it is highly unlikely that you need to worry. If not, set out for the vet's immediately. Untreated, distemper progresses to convulsions, motor disturbances, and often death.

Unfortunately, it does happen on occasion that the person from whom you got

If Your Dachshund Gets Sick

the puppy has neglected to have it vaccinated or has had it vaccinated with a passive vaccine that is only effective for three weeks. Active vaccines work only after the puppy is four weeks old, but they offer complete protection at that time. If a dog has been immunized with active vaccine, there should be a vaccination record by the administering veterinarian. Immunization against distemper must be repeated every one and one-half years.

Leptospirosis

This disease strikes primarily during the cool seasons of fall and winter, and male dogs are more susceptible than females. Symptoms include fever, loss of appetite, vomiting, lethargy, hindleg weakness, and, in serious cases, jaundice, foul mouth odors, and abnormal movements. Leptospirosis is a bacterial disease which can sometimes be cured by prompt treatment with antibiotics. A dog can be effectively protected against this disease, however, only through vaccination and appropriate booster shots.

Canine Hepatitis

This disease, which is caused by a virus, affects dogs of all ages, but puppies are more susceptible. Basically, an inflammation of the liver, it produces symptoms of fever, abdominal tenderness, diarrhea, and inflamed nasal and throat passages. Treatment with serum, antibiotics, replacement fluids, and vitamins may be effective, but many dogs that recover are left with eye problems that may lead to blindness. A

dog whose vaccinations are up to date basically cannot contract this disease, but you should still watch out that your dog does not drink water from muddy puddles and unclean streams—places where viruses and bacteria thrive.

Rabies

It is quite incomprehensible with what nonchalance some dog owners regard this terrible disease. Rabies is incurable; the progress of the disease is extremely painful and ends in death. Some owners are firmly convinced that their pets could not possibly have come in contact with animals that are affected, and they consequently neglect to have their dogs vaccinated.

Any dog can, without anyone's noticing it, come in contact with another animal that carries this disease. You might, for instance, take your dog for a walk in a park or in woods near the city. The dog wanders off the path and finds a dead rabbit, hare, weasel, or cat. Your dachshund sniffs the body before you notice and call it. It might already have picked up the disease. Or, it meets a stray dog on a walk, a dog that looks somewhat neglected but otherwise normal. How can you be sure that this stranger does not have rabies?

The rabies epidemic has spread so much since the mid-1960's that it is unlikely to be effectively combated soon. Sometimes it gets worse and sometimes it seems to recede, but basically it remains constant. Within a radius of about 12 miles (20 kilometers) of the town where I live in Holstein, Germany, six dogs had to be killed within one year because they were suspected of having contracted rabies. I heard of these six by chance; how many more lost their lives I do not know. All these dogs had had contact with other animals that were suspected of being rabid: foxes, cats, other wild animals, like martens, or other dogs. In every case, the dog's owner and any other persons who had contact with the dog had to undergo a very unpleasant and not altogether safe protective immunization.

Any unvaccinated dog that is under the slightest suspicion of having had contact with a rabid animal must be killed. You can avoid both the fear of catching rabies from your dog and the sorrow you would feel if your dog had to be put to sleep. A vaccination followed by yearly booster shots relieves us of all dangers.

I have discussed this topic at such length because the danger of rabies is so often minimized. Have your dachshund immunized against rabies even if you never leave the city; mice, rats, and cats are also carriers of this disease.

Protective Combination Vaccinations

Combination vaccines for distemper, infectious canine hepatitis, and leptospirosis have been available for some time. Now there is a combination vaccine that is effective against these three diseases as well as against rabies.

When should your dog be vaccinated? The so-called basic immunization of the puppy is normally taken care of by the breeder when the puppy is seven to nine weeks old. The seller must supply you, free of charge, with a proper vaccination record. The follow-up shots should be given when the puppy is twelve to fourteen weeks old. Let the veterinarian decide whether rabies should be included in this second immunization. The second round of shots are the responsibility of the puppy's new owner. Be sure to arrange for these shots at the right time.

Giving Medications

Dogs like some medications, and you should therefore see first whether your dachshund will take a medication without objection. If your dog won't take the pill straight, try wrapping the pill or capsule in a little chopped meat and offer it to the dog. It may gulp the pill down eagerly without even noticing anything strange. If it still refuses, you will have to resort to force. If you cannot control the dog by yourself, get another person to hold it still. This is how you introduce pills: open the dog's mouth by reaching one hand around the muzzle and forcing open the jaws. Place the pill as far back on the tongue as you can and then close the mouth and hold it shut with slight pressure. If you gently stroke the throat you will feel when your dachshund has swallowed the pill.

To introduce liquid medicine, carefully pull the side of the lower lip out to form a "pocket," pour the previously measured liquid into it, and raise the dog's head slightly. It will be forced to swallow. Be sure not to raise the head too much because then some of the liquid might literally go down the wrong tube.

If Your Dachshund Gets Sick

Can Dog Diseases Be Dangerous to Humans?

No doubt you would like to know whether infectious diseases affecting dogs can normally be communicated to humans. This is the case in one form of leptospirosis, but if the dog is vaccinated, there is no danger. Rabies can, of course, be transmitted—but only through biting.

If you are worried about toxoplasmosis, another viral disease, because you have read that this disease, which can endanger an unborn child, is sometimes transmitted by dogs, I can set your mind at ease. Dogs are not carriers of toxoplasmosis.

Euthanasia

Let me offer you some well-considered and serious thoughts on the subject of euthanasia. Prolonged illness and old age in humans often involve terrible suffering, and people are kept alive with the help of all kinds of machines, even in totally hopeless situations, if such a state can still be called life. Animals, on the other hand, can be released from their suffering painlessly if it is clear to the attending vet that help is no longer of any use and that nothing but pain is in store for them. I recommend that dog owners, out of love for their pet, do not ask their veterinarians to prolong its life and thus its suffering.

Dogs do not like going to see a doctor. Keep talking to your dachshund in reassuring tones during its examination.

Understanding Dachshunds

The History of Dachshunds

Research tells us that the wolf is the sole ancestor of all the different breeds of dogs. Wolves have long legs; we may therefore assume that all dogs at the time of their first domestication were long-legged, too.

Nature has its quirks, however, and sometimes plays havoc with the most ingenious and time-tested methods of breeding. A dumbfounded breeder may therefore find creatures in the whelping box that were neither anticipated nor wished for. Cairn terriers, for instance, occur in many colors ranging from reddish to sand and from gray to almost black, but white is not supposed to be one of their colors. In spite of this, white puppies appeared one day in an otherwise normal litter. The breeder culled these "miscolored" creatures, but Cairn terrier puppies with white fur turned up again and again, and it finally occurred to a breeder to turn this quirk of nature into a new breed of terrier, the West Highland white terrier.

I could list a number of similar examples. In science, such changes in nature are called mutations. A mutation is a sudden change in the hereditary material of an organism.

The shortening of the normally long legs of dogs must also have happened by way of mutation. Who knows, perhaps the first short-legged puppies were also culled at first, until it was realized that there were uses for short-legged dogs.

We have no idea when this happened, but color variations, short legs, and hanging ears are all the result of mutation. These changes were preserved because at some point there were some humans who liked the unplanned change in looks and perpetuated it. I would hesitate, though, to use the rather ambitious term "breeding" in the context of this early phase of our relationship with dogs.

In the past, dachshunds were bred primarily for hunting badgers and foxes. Their love of digging is a carry-over from those days.

There were already a number of different types of dogs, including short-legged ones, in existence at the time of early human civilization. In a rock tomb found in Beersheeba, Israel, which was then part of the Egyptian empire, a long-bodied, short-legged female dog with a pointed muzzle and erect ears is depicted. This tomb goes back to the period of the Middle Kingdom in the second millenium B.C. It is doubtful, though, that this Egyptian dog breed is

Understanding Dachshunds

a precursor of our dachshund; the short legs and long trunk are indeed reminiscent of a dachshund, but the muzzle and ears are more like those of a terrier. All this painting proves is that dogs with extremely long bodies and short legs already existed in ancient times.

The modern dachshund descends from hunting dogs found in western and central Europe. The breed's characteristics were standardized in Germany in 1879. Only eleven dachshunds were registered in the United States between 1879 and 1885, but in 1895, the Dachshund Club of America was officially recognized as part of the AKC.

Why Dachshunds are Bowlegged

It is impossible to reconstruct how dachshunds have acquired what have always struck me as pathologically bent front legs. This feature of dachshund anatomy is by now so firmly associated with the breed that some German writers often refer to the dachshund as *Krummbein* (bowlegs).

For a long time, breeders did nothing to correct the situation. On the contrary, the mistaken opinion prevailed that bent legs were an asset for digging into fox and rabbit burrows. Luckily for dachshunds, it was finally realized that their unnaturally bent legs were a hindrance rather than a help, and breeding goals were changed to obtain straight limbs. Of course, such a change cannot be accomplished in a day, and so there are still some dogs with "typical" dachshund legs, but fortunately for these charming creatures, not too many.

Vocal Expressions and Body Language

Every dog owner gradually learns to understand its dog's various vocal expressions. A bark can have a happy, angry, or melancholy ring. A dog can growl in warning, yelp with pain, howl in misery, or produce a soft purrlike rumble of pure bliss. The repertory of vocal expressions a mother uses with her puppies is even more varied.

A dachshund uses not only its voice but also its body to express itself. Just as we use gestures and facial expressions quite unconsciously, a dog also has a clear body language. You just have to understand it.

If a dog and a cat are introduced to each other early enough, they may become quite good friends.

Understanding Dachshunds

Just about everybody knows that a wagging tail expresses friendliness. You should not rely on this too much, however, and assume that a strnage dog is ready to be touched simply because it is wagging its tail. It may be "answering" your friendly words with tail wagging, but this does not imply that it will let you pet it unhindered. (Never pet a strange dog unless its owner gives explicit approval. This is a rule I want to stress, and you should be sure to teach it to your children.)

The play of the ears also expresses many things. Ears that are folded back always indicate that something is the matter. In older dogs, versed in human ways, this position of the ears can, in fact, express something like a bad conscience. The dog has done something that it knows from experience means trouble. A dog also folds its ears back with pleasure and excitement, but in that case, it will also wag its tail at the same time. In young, still inexperienced dogs, folded-back ears signal insecurity or fear. Pricked-up ears always indicate alertness.

If a dog shows its teeth, it does not necessarily mean it is about to bite; many dogs bare the teeth partially in a kind of "grin." According to my observations, there is always a small element of embarrassment in this. Let me give an example: I tell my dachshund to come because it has been scratching incessantly and I want to examine it. I think I have called in my normal tone, but somehow the dog has sensed something unusual. It agrees to come and even wags its tail, but at the same time it wears a strange little grin. Yawning, too, can be an expression of embarrassment.

If a dog walks on very stiff legs and raises the fur on its back as well, then extreme caution is in order. It is up to no good. It is not likely to approach humans in this threatening stance—though this does occur on occasion—but will display the stance toward a fellow dog that is not to its liking. Raised lips that expose all the teeth is an extreme danger signal that means this dog will bite without hesitation.

I should like to say a few words about dogs that bite out of fear. A self-confident dog with a strong character has no need to take on a threatening stance, let alone attack. A timid, fearful dog, however, is constantly petrified that someone might hurt it and consequently bites more or less indiscriminately whenever a dog or human gets too close. Paradoxically, such a dog may acquire the reputation of being ferocious and a good watchdog, but in reality there is nothing but fear behind its aggressiveness.

Dachshunds have unusually expressive eyes. Their facial expressions reflect a wide range of moods from pleasure—even anticipatory pleasure—to pain and grief, as well as fighting spirit, pride, impatience, guilt, devotion, and last but not least, hurt feelings.

So, always observe a dog's posture carefully; its body speaks a very clear language.

The Typical Dachshund

A Dog with Character

Many people think that dachshunds are self-willed, obstinate, and never learn to obey. This view is as firmly lodged in some people's heads as the association between dachshunds and bowlegs.

I have run into quite a few obnoxious dachshunds. Their owners would inevitably explain to me at length that since dachshunds are impossible to train there was no point in trying. This attitude is just as amazing as the reaction of many other people who express surprise at how well my dachshunds behave. "How on earth do you do it?" I have been asked a number of times. The answer is very simple. It never even occurs to me that one of my dachshunds might refuse to obey me. Of course, I have had some dachshunds that let themselves be trained without major effort on my part and others that demanded all the persistence and energy I had to make them understand that *I* was "top dog." I find nothing surprising in this; dachshunds are living creatures with a strongly developed character.

Independence, or what could be called obstinacy, is deeply rooted in the dachshund's character. Our little friend needs this quality; it is essential to its survival. After all, the dachshund, or "badger dog," was originally used for hunting, in which it performed a very specific task. When a dachshund was sent digging underground to drive a badger or fox from its burrow, it was a matter of life and death. It requires great courage and iron determination to accomplish this task. No human can come to its aid when it is down there, and it must rely completely on itself. It takes a strong will to embark on—and succeed at—such a venture time and again. This hunting background is also responsible for another typi-

cal dachshund trait—its propensity for digging holes or scratching at the floor as if digging.

In their "nonprofessional" lives—that is, in their role as family dogs—dachshunds of strong character will also try to get to the head of the pack. The "pack" in this case is made up of the members of its human family. In the chapter on training (page 58), I will show that it is indeed possible to train them, if we understand their character, maintain our own will, and proceed with patience and consistency.

Minor Annoyances

I once raised a litter of Great Danes in a small apartment. There were six puppies, and needless to say, they caused quite a bit of trouble. This was nothing compared with the havoc raised by three dachshund puppies I had later, even though they had a whole house and a garden to romp around in. One time, for instance, they managed to remove half the floor covering in a large

If you do not train your dachshunds with consistency right from the start, you must be prepared for unending mischief.

kitchen strip by strip in no time at all. Another time, they peeled most of the wallpaper off the walls in the dining area. To be sure, other puppies may be up to similar tricks, but I have found that dachshund puppies far outstrip others in their imagination for mischief.

When we come upon scenes like this it is very hard to keep a sense of humor. Ultimately we have nobody but ourselves to blame. We should leave the playful little imps alone only in places that offer them no temptation.

Bosom friends: two of the author's dogs.

Several years ago I decided to get a female wirehaired dachshund as a companion for my Great Dane. I had been interested in this strain of dachshund for some time, and choosing this particular dog proved a stroke of luck. I doubt I ever wept more tears over a dog than I did when I had to have her put to sleep because she was suffering from an incurable cancer when she was thirteen years old.

My dog, Gümperle, was a perfect dog: good-natured, friendly even toward other animals, obedient without a trace of obsequiousness, and very alert and watchful. She was totally devoted to me. To be sure, she was also fond of my husband, but he was away quite a lot. When he was home on weekends and wanted to go for a walk with the dogs, the Great Dane would always be ready to go along happily, but not the little dachshund. She would indicate very clearly, "I am not going anywhere without my mistress!" and there was no convincing her otherwise. When I went away on trips, my husband had to look after the dogs. At these times Gümperle would go on daytime walks without hesitating. At night, though, when the dogs had to go out once more, Gümperle was not inclined to cooperate. Particularly in bad weather, she failed to recognize the necessity of going out again and would try to turn around and slip back into the house. It took my husband several days to catch on to her. She would leave the house with the other dogs, and head for the garden, but then she would quickly disappear into the shadows and wait until my husband was not paying attention. Then she would dash back to the house behind his back. My husband was always amazed that Gümperle was already inside by the time the other two returned. Eventually he caught on to her, and then she had to go out and do her business together with the other dogs. This she did without objection once she realized that he had seen through

Understanding Dachshunds

her trick. Cleverness and an amazingly playful mischievousness are simply part of the dachshund's personality. These are also the qualities that make us love them in spite of the little annoyances that they sometimes cause.

Almost all dachshunds, but especially young ones, like to make off with objects that arouse their interest. It may be a shoe, a potholder, or almost anything else. They carry their trophy off with a look of great triumph. Sometimes it is not easy to keep from bursting into laughter when watching them and to demand firmly that the booty be relinquished. Consistent training is essential to discourage a dachshund from such behavior.

An acquaintance of mine whose dachshund had a special predilection for paper soon found this out. Whenever the dog had a chance it would snap up any piece of paper and disappear underneath a bench. There he would reduce it to confetti before being lured out. By the time this habit could be broken he had destroyed a number of letters, some medical prescriptions, and even a check.

Dachshunds like the comforts of lying on soft things, preferably on upholstered armchairs and couches. If they are not allowed to do this but are reluctant to give up the habit, a prolonged battle of will between dog and master can ensue. I know of a dachshund, for instance, who—in spite of the most energetic "No's" and occasional smacks—persisted in jumping up on a favorite chair. Its master had always succeeded in training his dachshunds, but in this instance he finally had to resort to a compromise. He had a carpenter build him a sturdy platform with four legs at about the height of a chair. This he equipped with some padding and put in place of the dog's sleeping basket. The dachshund first regarded this new object with curiosity, then with the tilt of the head that signifies suspicion. Finally it jumped up, turned in a circle a few times, then settled down, accepting "its chair."

Training Your Dachshund Properly

Training Is Necessary

A dog's behavior, despite its breed characteristics, is largely determined by the training it receives as a puppy and young dog. Only a well-behaved dog is a real joy, and only an obedient dog can be relied upon. Lack of training also exposes a dog to dangers, especially in traffic, and in the countryside a dog that runs loose after game may be shot by a hunter or game warden. A lot of effort should therefore be put into training from the very beginning—particularly in the case of dachshunds, who are famous for having wills of their own.

You can start teaching your puppy the rudiments of good dog behavior from the

Do not expect your dachshund puppy to take to walking on a leash the first day.

day it arrives. You cannot expect that the little creature will take to collar and leash without protest, walk obediently next to you, or be house-broken right away. Presumably it was able up to now to relieve itself at will, without worrying about where it was done. Now, all of a sudden, it may be yanked up with a scream of horror. Perhaps the inexperienced dog owner even rubs the poor creature's nose in the puddle. Such attempts at "training" are cruel and examples of how *not* to approach training.

My own approach to training will be discussed in two stages: the first covering the basic rules and second covering more advanced obedience techniques.

The First Stage of Training: Basic Rules

During the first stage, the puppy must be taught with much patience what is expected of it from its human family. It must learn what is acceptable and what is unacceptable. It learns this by trial and error, and naturally not all its experiences or yours will be of a pleasant nature. A puppy that grew up as part of the breeder's family is obviously at an advantage over one that was raised purely in a kennel because it is already familiar with the basic rules of good dog behavior, but it, too, is still of "preschool" age. To make matters worse, you are probably speaking the equivalent of a foreign language because you are using different words from the ones it is accustomed to hearing from the breeder. So please do not expect your puppy to know the rules without giving it time to learn.

Training Your Dachshund Properly

It is the tone that counts. Dachshunds are extremely willful, and their feelings are easily hurt if they feel unjustly treated.

One Word for One Thing

You can make learning a lot easier if you decide at the very beginning to use one and the same word for any one process. This is the only way a young dog can learn what human sounds mean. Words are not concepts to dogs but only meaningless sounds; dogs have their own ways to convey meaning—namely, barking, yowling, whining, and growling.

For example, if you want your dog to go to its bed you have to say "bed" every time. If you repeat this consistently, it will soon connect the sound "bed" with its sleeping place. At the beginning you will have to lead it to its bed, but at some point

the moment will come when it goes all by itself upon hearing the word. How long it takes to get to this point depends on its intelligence and your quiet persistence.

Here is the first important rule for this stage of training: *Always use the same word for the same process. It does not matter what word it is; just make sure you always use the same one.*

Responding Immediately

You must teach your dog not only things you like it to do but also what you don't like it to do. How is the dog to know that chewing on furniture or electrical wires is off limits, that carpets are not to be shredded, and that it may sharpen its teeth on only a few selected items? You must find a way of spoiling its pleasure in these undesirable activities. "Punishment" is not appropriate here because it presupposes knowledge of wrongdoing. Nevertheless, the young dog must come to understand, "If I chew on this rug, something unpleasant is going to happen to me, so I had better not do it." This "something unpleasant" obviously must emanate from you, and there should be an immediate and direct connection between it and the deed. Only then will the dog understand that chewing on rugs is unacceptable and will, with some luck, give it up soon.

If the dog does something naughty in your absence, neither cries of horror nor scolding will do any good. It has no idea why you are suddenly yelling. It can tell well enough by the tone of your voice that you are angry, but it is beyond it to grasp that there is any connection between your

Training Your Dachshund Properly

vociferous outburst and some activity it has long since forgotten. It will think that your anger was aroused by what it is doing at the moment. Perhaps it has only been playing with its ball as you have encouraged it to do. If your dog slinks off with a downcast look, it is not suffering from a bad conscience! It is merely making itself scarce because instinct tells it that it is better to stay out of the way of an angry "pack leader."

So remember: praise and rebuke should only follow immediately on the heels of the action you want to encourage or discourage. Young dogs in particular can associate only things that are closely connected in time.

Thus, the second important rule of the first stage of training is: *Praise or rebuke right after the dog's action to indicate the connection between the action and the response.*

The Right Tone of Voice

In training, the tone of voice plays a crucial role. Words in themselves are meaningless at first, but the dog will react instinctively to the tone in which they are voiced. If you speak in a too friendly and gentle way, it will feel happy if you are praising it, but it probably won't obey if you use the same tone. If you say the same words in a too harsh or clipped way, or perhaps a little louder than usual, it will be startled. My dogs, for instance, learn very early that a short but firm "no!" is a prohibition that is to be respected under all circumstances. If I had said "no" in a soft and friendly way, the word would have

lost all its efficacy. The dogs would inevitably have concluded that this gentle "no" was merely pleasant conversation.

So here is the third rule of this training stage: *Praise in gentle tones; scold in firm tones.*

A dachshund puppy learns dog behavior in the course of play with its siblings.

Learning Through Play

In the section Training Starts Early (page 37), I mentioned that animal parents naturally and playfully teach their offspring how to behave.

Our puppies, too, can learn a lot through games. This is a pleasant method for introducing a puppy to some exercises that it may not like at first. Games are particularly useful in getting a puppy accustomed to the leash (page 66) and to the commands "let go" (page 67), "sit," and "come." It will also learn to fetch quickly if you call out the command at just the moment it is playing with its ball or rawhide bone. You will soon notice that your little dog likes to learn this way and is full of enthusiasm.

Training Your Dachshund Properly

The last basic rule of this first phase of training, then, is this: *Teach your dog as much as you possibly can in play situations. Pleasant experiences enhance its readiness to obey.*

Discipline Techniques

In the first stage of training you should not even think in terms of punishment; think of your actions as a form of "behavior modification" instead. The spanking may feel the same to the dog, but the distinction is meant to aid you in thinking of yourself less as a dispenser of punishment than as a good teacher. How does a good teacher get this message across to a four-legged pupil?

I grew up with dogs, and their company has been as natural to me since I was a small child as the air I breathe. I do not remember a single disobedient dog at my parents' home. After I was married, I had a dog of my own for the first time, and I trained it the way I had seen at home.

Later I read many books that dealt with the proper training of dogs. From these books I learned that the method I had followed was apparently not correct. When a dog did something it was not supposed to do I had always promptly tapped it on the rump and exclaimed loudly, "no!" The dog would stop very quickly. My action had the desired effect. Then, however, I read that one should not hit a dog with the hand because this made it afraid of hands. Instead you were supposed to quickly fold a newspaper in half and spank it lightly

with that. That made sense to me, even though I had not noticed that my dogs were at all shy of hands.

When the next puppy arrived at our house, I decided to resist "handing" out instant justice. Whenever I came upon some mischief, I would quickly grab a newspaper. The dog would look up at me and stop whatever it was doing. The only problem was that by the time I had found and folded my newspaper it was often not doing what had aroused my displeasure.

Punishment must follow on the heels of the crime, or the dachshund puppy will fail to make any connection between the two events.

Then I had a surprise. One day, after my husband had been playing with the puppy, he reached for his newspaper to read it, whereupon the little fellow made for its bed with great haste. It had learned to be scared of newsapers. I realized that this method of training had led to some misunderstandings. Something was going wrong, as this incident showed. For one thing, too much time had elapsed between the undesirable act and its consequence. It also seemed to me that the newspaper was too "foreign," whereas the dog had no trouble immediately understanding and accepting the spank of the hand given at the right moment. I consequently returned to my old method, and I have never yet had a badly behaved dog or one that shied away from human hands.

There is another method of disciplining puppies that has been recommended recently. You are supposed to grab the dog by the scruff of the neck and shake it. This is said to be "in keeping with the nature of dogs" because a puppy's mother supposedly treats it this way.

I cannot subscribe to this. I have never yet observed a mother disciplining her puppies in this fashion. If a puppy arouses her displeasure, she growls or snaps at it. Perhaps one dog will do this to a weaker opponent in a fight, but that is not a matter of training but rather of overpowering a rival.

There is another reason I am opposed to this type of treatment. The fur on the nape of a dog's neck is not made for lifting. It is not good for a puppy to be yanked up this way, even though some of them suffer it without expressing pain. If you handle your puppy this roughly whenever it does something you don't want it to, you may be hurting it too seriously, too often. A quick smack that startles more than it hurts suffices.

What if it is not possible to administer discipline right after the puppy has been naughty. If, for instance, it has been chewing on its toy and we suddenly notice from a distance that the toy has been abandoned in favor of a chair leg, it is hard to deliver the tap the moment it is needed. By the time we get close it will have noticed us and stopped chewing to greet our approach joyfully. Here it is best to call out a loud and energetic "no!" and maybe clap our hands the moment we see the puppy at the chair. If it becomes startled and forgets the chair leg, at least the chair will be safe, and the "no" may register. Obviously the most effective way is to give a smack before it knows what is happening. Say "no!" at the same time loudly and sharply. The smack does not have to be hard. Do this whenever the puppy does anything you want to break it of. As soon as it has stopped, you must praise it. Let me say once more, never forget the reprimanding "no" when you train your puppy not to do something. After a while this word alone will do the trick.

The four most important things a puppy must learn as soon as possible are to be house-broken, to stay in its own place on command, to walk on leash, and to obey the command, "let go!"

Housebreaking

When your dachshund puppy arrives at home, the first problem to tackle is housebreaking. This will be more difficult if you live in an apartment. If all you need to do is open the door to the yard, the problem is easily dealt with. You simply have to be quick to prevent your puppy from emptying its bladder indoors. If it has already urinated, there is little sense in taking it out

Take your dachshund puppy outside as often as possible during the first days to avoid accidents.

after the fact. The challenge is to catch it *before* and take it to the proper spot. This means, of course, that you should watch it carefully and recognize by its behavior when it needs to go. Basically a dog, especially a puppy or young dog, should be taken outside in the morning as soon as it wakes up. It is bound to have to relieve itself then. It will also have to go after naps, and young dogs nap often in the course of a day. That it should go out after meals is obvious. This means that you need the time and patience to take your puppy out quite a few times. The greatest trick is to recognize the magic moment in a dog that is playing (remember, we are still talking about *young* dogs). When it suddenly stops playing and starts sniffing around with its nose to the ground, the utmost speed is in order. Sometimes this signal is omitted because the puppy, like a small child who is totally absorbed in some game, may empty its bladder quite unconsciously. The more consistent you are and the better you watch, the sooner the puppy will learn to indicate on its own that it wants to go out. Soon the habit will be so ingrained that you can relax your vigilance.

Bowel movements present fewer problems. They occur at most two or three times a day and at fairly regular times. Once you have figured out your dog's habits, you should take it out at the appropriate times and walk it until it has done its business.

The more time you have for your dog at the beginning, the easier it will become house-broken. What about a dog that lives in an upstairs apartment? How can you get it outside in time? This is almost impossible in a high-rise apartment. Perhaps you can succeed in the morning if you are up in time and rush downstairs with your dog under your arm. You cannot let it walk downstairs or sit in the elevator because it would immediately try to squat and empty its bladder. You will have to carry it from its bed to the street outside.

What do you do during the day? You have no choice but to set up an area for "paper" training. This has several disadvantages, but may be the only solution. A thick layer of newspaper in a shallow plastic pan or on the floor can serve the purpose. Carry the puppy to the pan when you think it needs to go, hold it there, encouraging it with gentle words, and wait until it does. Then you have to shower it with praise. Gradually the young dog will grasp what is expected and go to the designated spot on its own. Needless to say, this spot has to be accessible at all times; the dog should never be confronted with a closed door. The newspaper should, of course, be replaced after it has been used. This solution may seem eminently practical, but it has one major disadvantage: once a dog has formed a habit, it is very hard to change it. A puppy that has learned only to use a newspaper will urinate only in this one spot at home, but what are you going to do when you are out with it all day or have to take it on a trip? Get your puppy accustomed both to using a newspaper indoors and to relieving itself outside—always in the same spot wherever it is allowed by local ordinances. This is usually off the sidewalk in the gutter and not in public parks.

Staying In Its Place

If the spot for the dog's bed is well chosen (page 24), your dog will happily retire there once it has grasped that this is *its* place. After it has had a first thorough look around its new environment and shows some signs of being tired, take it to the carton or basket and hold it there—if necessary with some force—while talking to it in a flattering way and repeating the word *bed* in an emphatic tone several times. Once it settles down, you should walk away. If it gets up and leaves the bed, take it back right away and keep re-

peating the word *bed*. You must do this ever so gently and lovingly; otherwise, it will be afraid. Even at this early stage your patience and persistence are the key to success. Since dogs generally seek out a secluded corner to sleep in, getting a puppy used to its sleeping place usually does not take very long.

Walking on a Leash

A dog tht is kept in a city has to learn to walk on a leash right away. If it has never worn a collar before and has never experienced the restriction to its freedom of movement that a leash exerts, it will submit to this procedure only under duress.

A dachshund puppy should not perceive his collar and leash as a restriction of freedom. Get it used to them in play.

Training Your Dachshund Properly

Never let things come to the point where the dog fights the leash in desperation. Then it will be so frightened by the increased pressure on its throat from pulling that it will only struggle more, thereby increasing the pressure and terror even more.

Start the training by carrying the puppy to the street and putting it down with its leash on. Now, let *it* lead *you,* not the other way round. Avoid the slightest tension on the leash. If the leash does begin to tighten and your dachshund starts to panic, give in to its pulling, keeping the leash loose (but never let go of it), and talk to your dog soothingly. Try to lure it closer to you; usually this is not too difficult because young puppies that have just been separated from their mothers are eager for contact. They seek humans and like to snuggle up close.

To teach the puppy as quickly as possible that collar and leash are not instruments of torture, it also helps to play with them first at home. Put the collar and leash on and then encourage it to come up to you. Let it chew and yank on the leash if it wants to (you can break it of this habit later). The dog has to get the feeling that the leash is a link to its master rather than a hated means of oppression.

As soon as it comes up to you, you should praise and pet it so that it learns, "Going up to my master (or mistress) is good." This is one of the most important realizations a young dachshund must come to. If it is dead set against responding to the leash and resists violently in spite of all your cajoling, you must pull it closer to you very gently, saying soothing things to it, like "That's a good dog," all the while.

When it is finally next to you, you should give it a little treat as a reward. If you follow this method, just about any puppy will soon adjust to collar and leash.

As soon as it has gotten used to walking on the leash, you must make sure that it is not the dog that walks you—that is, pulls you along behind. Break it of this habit if necessary by yanking the leash back firmly and calling something like "back!" sharply at the same time. The yank and the call will startle the dog, and it will automatically stop a moment, for which you should naturally give praise. Be sure to stop every attempt at pulling.

There are two more things I want to say in connection with taking a dog out. Never let a young dog off the leash if you have to take it out on streets with traffic. And, always see to it that your dog does its business where local ordinances indicate. In some localities a dog owner must clear away the dog's bowel movements.

The Command "Let Go"

Every dog—including the dachshund—has to learn to accept that people may take things away from it. "Let go" is the appropriate command for this, and it must be spoken loudly and emphatically. It may, of course, happen that your dog is not at all agreeable to this and defends its food, toy, or other "booty" by growling. From the dog's point of view, this is a perfectly logical reaction. When it was a little puppy it had to assert itself against its siblings or it would soon have been reduced to the role of underdog—that is, the member of the

Training Your Dachshund Properly

pack that is victimized by all the others. It is quite often comical to watch a little midget of a dog challenge a human being, as most dogs with character will try to do, but you should never let it have its way. A dachshund knows instantly when it has the upper hand. After that it will never let anyone take anything away from it again. The dog must recognize that it is up against somebody stronger-willed and that it had better yield to this stronger creature. If it growls when you take away its food dish, scold it with an emphatic "no!" If it responds with more growling and perhaps by snapping at you, give it a swift swat that it can feel (the most effective place is on the side of the muzzle). If this makes it even angrier, which is quite within the realm of possibility, grab it firmly on the back of

At the command "Let go!" the dachshund knows that it must drop whatever it has in its mouth right away.

the neck and scold it in a loud voice. As soon as it gives in, praise it with many kind words and give its food back.

Practice this daily! It is almost impossible to teach this lesson to a grown dog without its resulting in serious biting. You should also practice taking away a toy. If it does not want to relinquish it immediately, reach your hand over its nose and gently pry the jaws apart. As you do this, say in an admonitory but kind tone, "Let go!" As soon as it drops the toy, give the toy back to the dog and praise it. Almost any young dachshund soon learns to enjoy this game and readily drops whatever it has between its teeth at the command "let go." Later on it will do this when you call from a distance, but this only works if the puppy has learned to obey the command without the slightest hesitation.

Let me give you another good reason for learning this lesson. Every dog occasionally picks up something that it should not swallow. If the correct reaction to the command "let go" has become deeply ingrained, it will obey even if it is at some distance from you, and it will drop the object.

Somebody might object at this point that a dachshund is bound to lose its personality if it is constantly forced to subordinate itself. This is not the case. A dachshund will stay the same dachshund even if it has to learn to submit to a will stronger than its own. For the dachshund, obeying and submitting is as natural as the attempt to fill the role of "top dog." Unfortunately, there are some dogs whose masters have beaten all the character out of them, dogs that are literally filled with nothing but fear and

68

come crawling on their bellies when they are called. They are pitiable creatures indeed, and people who vent their lust for power on dogs because they have no place else to express it should be forbidden by law to keep dogs.

The Second Phase of Training

Obedience Training

What we wish for in a dog and aim to achieve through our training efforts is to make of it an obedient and agreeable companion, a four-legged friend. It is supposed to keep its cheerful disposition—but it does have to obey.

When a young dachshund has grasped the first lessons of training already discussed and has learned to respond correctly to the basic commands addressed to it, the first phase of its education is complete. To review, it should announce when it has to go out, it should walk properly on a leash, and it should go to its bed and stay there when given the command. The dog must also relinquish what it has in its mouth promptly and without resistance when asked. At this point it has passed the basic course of training and can now go on to more complex tasks.

At this second stage of its education your dachshund should be able to learn whatever you want to teach it. It should be able, for example, to run free off the leash—in appropriate surroundings—and come bounding back promptly and happily when you call or whistle for it. This, too, will not happen overnight, especially if you try to teach it when your dog is six or

seven months old and goes through a stage of adolescent rebellion. From the moment my dachshunds were allowed to run without a leash, I have always praised them lavishly and rewarded them with a little treat every time they came back to me when I called. As soon as they realized that coming back meant getting something good to eat, they would come dashing up in happy anticipation. This did not change even as the treats became smaller and were gradually replaced by mere words of loving praise. Before you reach that point, however, your dachshund may drive you nearly to distraction when it refuses to pay the slightest attention to all your calling and whistling. When it finally decides to come

If your training efforts are not successful in every instance, look for the fault in yourself and not your dachshund.

Training Your Dachshund Properly

back, you must muster all the self-control you have to praise it. If you let your anger out and scold it because of its disobedience or even hit it with the leash, it will be worse the next time because in its doggy head it will reason something like, "When I came back I got a beating. So I had better take my time or, better yet, not come back at all. Just look at how mad my pack leader gets!"

Who Trains Whom?

In conclusion I would like to offer a few thoughts. It takes a lot of consistency—and that means time and patience—to turn an inexperienced puppy into a pleasant companion for home and outings. It is because only a well-trained dog ensures a happy and smooth coexistence between human and dog that I have devoted this much space to the important topic of training a dachshund.

Up to now I have focused on how to train a dachshund as intelligently and with as much regard for its nature as possible, but I have often wondered privately to what extent my dachshunds have trained me and still do.

Take the time to think about how living with a dachshund has gradually changed your ways. How if, in the past, you regarded the idea of "order" somewhat nonchalantly, your dog has taught you to become more meticulous in this area, perhaps by chewing on shoes or whatever else is left standing or lying around. Or how punctual you have become because your dog must be taken out at a certain hour. Without our being aware of it, our "well-trained, obedient" dachshund has as subtly modified our behavior as we have its.

Sources of Information

American Kennel Club
51 Madison Avenue
New York, New York 10010

Australian Kennel Club
Royal Show Grounds
Ascot Vale, Victoria
Australia

British Kennel Club
1 Charles Street
Picadilly, London W. 1
England

Canadian Kennel Club
2150 Bloor Street West
Toronto, Ontario
Canada

Dachshund Club of America
c/o Mrs. William Burr Hill
2031 Lake Shore Boulevard
Jacksonville, Florida 32210

Index

Index

Nose, 16
Nursing, *28*, 37
Nursing toxemia, 37
Nutrition, 40–41

Obedience, 69–70
Obstinacy, 5, 55
Offspring, 37, 39, 60

Pack, living in, 55
Panting, 33
Paralysis, 47–48
Parasites, 47
Parasite infestation, 31
Paws, 19, 22
Pedigrees, 7
Permission to breed, 38
Pet dealers, 9
Physical Make-up, 16, 19–20
Play, 10, 60
Plume, 15
Poisoning, 47
Pregnancy, 36
Protective vaccinations, 48–50
Puppies, 8–11
Purity of bread, 7, 12, 38

Quarantine, 32
Quarantine regulations, 32

Rabies, 49–50
Rabies vaccination, 50
Raw pork, 42
Roundworm, 47

Safety measures, 33–34
Scent, 16
Scratching, 43
Settling in, 29
Shedding season, 43
Short legs, 52
Short-haired dachshund
  (smooth), *frontispiece, 45*
Signs of illness, 43–44
Sleeping place, 24, 66
Sleeping basket, 24
Slipped disk, 6, 47–48

Smooth dachshund (short-
  haired)
Spanking, 61–62
Spaying, 36
Standard, 16, 19–20
Studs, 36
Surgery, 48

Tail, 54
Tail wagging, 54
Tapeworm, 47
Teeth, 32
Temperature, taking of, 44
Temperature, 44
Test of all-around skills
Ticks, 31
"Tiger" dachshund, *64*
Toenail clippers, 25
Toenails, 31–32
Toes, 19
Tongue, 16
Toxoplasmosis, 51
Toys, 25–26
Trailing by sound
Training, 37–38, 58–62,
  65–70
Training trials
Travel, 32–34
Trials, hunting (utility)

Urinating, 65–66
Utility dogs

Vaccination record, 50
Value of purebreds, 13
Vocal expression, 53–54
Vomiting, 44, 47

Walks, 66–67
Water dish, 24
Whelping, 37
Whipworm, 47
Wirehaired dachshund, *17*, 21,
  45, 46
Worm infestation, 47

Yawning, 54